"Jennie Allen not only casts an incredible vision for true friendship and community, but she also leads the way by example. In an age when we're tempted to believe deep and meaningful friendships are impossible, *Find Your People* is a timely, practical resource."

—RUTH CHOU SIMONS, *Wall Street Journal* bestselling author, artist, and founder of gracelaced.com

"Deep community is the path to health, joy, success, connection. *Find Your People* will inspire you, challenge you, and encourage you toward the relationships you need and want."

—ANNIE F. DOWNS, *New York Times* bestselling author of *That Sounds Fun*

"Every generation must learn again for the first time that the fathomless ache we all experience is that of being alone— and that the trinitarian God of the Bible has come in Jesus to heal the ache and recommission us for the work of creating beauty and goodness in the world. For this generation Jennie Allen is the vulnerable voice we need, and with *Find Your People* she has provided a beacon-illuminated map that is as practical as it is inspiring. Read this and find your people. Read this and find the life you have been hungering and thirsting for. Read this and find Jesus."

—CURT THOMPSON, MD, author of *The Soul of Desire* and *The Soul of Shame*

"We were never designed to journey through life alone. We need to be seen, to be known, and to belong in order to flourish. In *Find Your People,* Jennie Allen shows us how to build deeper, stronger relationships that point us to Jesus and help us live out our God-given purpose."

—CHRISTINE CAINE, speaker, author, and founder of Propel Women

"Community is key to living a full and faith-filled life. Jennie Allen does a beautiful job of using her own journey to give us a vision for why we need people in our lives and, more important, how we can find those people. This book is going to challenge you to say no to the lies of the enemy and find what I call your circle of faith. *Find Your People* will inspire you not only to find those who will fight on your behalf but also to become a fighter for the people in your life."

—MICHAEL TODD, lead pastor of Transformation Church and *New York Times* bestselling author of *Relationship Goals* and *Crazy Faith*

BOOKS BY JENNIE ALLEN

Get Out of Your Head:
Stopping the Spiral of Toxic Thoughts

Nothing to Prove: Why We Can Stop Trying So Hard

Made for This: 40 Days to Living Your Purpose

Anything: The Prayer That Unlocked
My Good and My Soul

Restless: Because You Were Made for More

Stuck: The Places We Get Stuck and
the God Who Sets Us Free

Chase Study: Chasing After the Heart of God

FIND YOUR PEOPLE

FIND YOUR PEOPLE

· · · ·

BUILDING DEEP COMMUNITY IN A LONELY WORLD

· · ·

Jennie Allen

WATERBROOK

LIBRARY OF CONGRESS CATALOGING-IN-PUBLICATION DATA

NAMES: Allen, Jennie, author.
TITLE: Find your people : building deep community in a lonely world / Jennie Allen.
DESCRIPTION: First edition. | [Colorado Springs, Colorado] : WaterBrook, [2022] | Includes bibliographical references.
IDENTIFIERS: LCCN 2021029667 | ISBN 9780593193389 (hardcover) | ISBN 9780593193396 (ebook)
SUBJECTS: LCSH: Interpersonal relations—Religious aspects—Christianity. | Communities—Religious aspects—Christianity. | Friendship— Religious aspects—Christianity.
CLASSIFICATION: LCC BV4597.52 .A45 2022 | DDC 158.2—dc23
LC record available at https://lccn.loc.gov/2021029667

Printed in the United States of America on acid-free paper

waterbrookmultnomah.com

2 4 6 8 9 7 5 3 1

First Edition

Dedicated to my village of friends.

———

THANKS FOR MAKING ME BETTER.

THANKS FOR FIGHTING FOR ME.

THANKS FOR STAYING.

It is not good for man to be alone.

—GOD, AFTER HE BUILT THE
FIRST HUMAN ON EARTH

———

So, as messy as relationships might be,

we cannot live life alone.

We have to figure this out.

CONTENTS

■

WE AREN'T SUPPOSED
TO BE THIS LONELY

■

I HAD A PANIC ATTACK LAST WEEK. A FULL-FLEDGED, COULDN'T-catch-my-breath, on-the-floor-of-my-closet panic attack. I haven't had one in ten years.

I write these words with the rest of this book nearly finished. And yet I want to be honest with you: this is my reality today, after spending a couple years of my life living, writing, researching, and thinking about something that apparently at least three in five of us feel daily:

Loneliness.

I imagine you are here because you feel it too. That sinking feeling that you aren't seen, you aren't known, and you are on your own to face whatever difficult thing life is throwing at you.

I get it.

But I'm convinced that feeling is rooted in a big fat lie—a

lie that threatens to pull you and me into a dark place unless we learn how to fight back.

Case in point: my recent panic attack.

IT HAD BEEN BUILDING over the course of several weeks.

I'd hidden myself away to edit this book, and when I finally emerged . . .

. . . I was in a fight with one of my sisters. We hadn't seen each other in months, and we both live so busy. But my sisters are two of my closest friends.

. . . My husband was frustrated that I had been so disconnected, because even when I wasn't working on the book, I was distracted by the million things that had fallen to the wayside.

. . . I realized my people had been building memories together and sharing experiences without me. It had been so long since I was available to hang out, they had finally stopped calling. In my mind they had moved on together, and I was now alone on the outside.

All this hit at once, along with this crushing certainty: while I was writing a book about finding your people, I lost all of mine.

I was a complete fraud. I didn't have people.

The conflict, isolation, and fear went on for weeks. And it kept growing. I thought about it all the time. Then, after yet another person expressed disappointment in me, I found myself alone on my closet floor, unable to catch my breath. The lie that left me gasping?

———

I am all alone.

That same night I had a vivid nightmare in which my worst fears came true. My people were not only quitting me, they were gossiping about me, stabbing me in the back—and I had a book out in the world about how close we all were.

Drama, I know. I imagine you're now wondering about what kind of help you can expect from someone who was recently melting down over this very topic.

So why tell you this?

Because on some deep level, being alone is a fear we all share.

Maybe you're experiencing loneliness right now?

Maybe you had people and they quit you?

Or maybe you've never truly had your people?

Or maybe you have them, but even when you're with them, you feel distant and unseen?

THE ACHE OF LONELINESS is real, and it's haunting us.

I mentioned in *Get Out of Your Head* that my neuro-buddy Curt Thompson likes to say we all come into the world looking for someone looking for us. It's true, but it's incomplete; we are looking for more than that.

In a recent conversation about connection, Curt pointed me to these three words we need from infant to ninety![1]

Every human is looking to be:

———

Seen
  Soothed
  Safe

We don't just want to be seen; we want to tell a friend or loved one about our disappointments and hopes and find comfort as well.

We want to be seen and comforted, and we want to be safe. But we aren't always safe.

We aren't always comforted, and it might feel like we aren't even seen.

Sometimes it's as simple as a fleeting thought. You're falling asleep with some worries about your future, and this whisper sneaks into your mind: *No one even knows what I'm going through.*

Sometimes it's a deeper reality: life has been so chaotic and stressful for so many years that you accidentally didn't invest in your relationships, and when you look up, your people are gone.

It's a profound, in-the-crevices-of-our-souls sense of isolation.

It's the wondering if you are truly known, seen, accepted, even cherished, such as when:

- You don't know whom to call to pick you up at the airport.
- You have something to celebrate or grieve and no one to celebrate or grieve with.

- You have an idea you want to brainstorm and can't think of anyone who would care enough to dream with you.
- You're dealing with a difficult situation at work but can't think of anyone safe you can talk it through with.
- Most of your friend group is married and starting to have kids, and you aren't even dating.
- Your kids are grown, and you are single and spend most of your time alone.
- You are eating another meal alone—again.
- You are looking at the weekend and don't have a single plan. Unless you initiate or go it alone, you won't have anything to do.
- You're talking to someone you thought was a good friend but realize you are on completely different pages about important issues.
- Your family is broken and unhealthy, when it seems everyone else is excited to be going home to see their (normal, happy, well-adjusted) families at Christmas.
- You need to talk but don't know whom to call.
- You haven't had anyone genuinely listen to you in so long that you honestly can't remember the last time you opened up.

These scenes strike at the quiet ache I'm talking about. It's just an inescapable reality of the human condition, right? Isn't it just something we all face?

Or is it just me?

Or is it just *you*?

Do you ever wonder that? If maybe you're the only person who feels *this* alone?

You aren't, by the way.

You aren't alone in feeling alone.

The morning after that vivid nightmare, I woke up and saw with crystal clarity:

I am believing the lie that I'm destined to be alone, and in believing that lie I'm making it into reality, because I am pulling back and judging those I love, guarding myself from them as if *they* were the enemies.

It was early but even as I was having that thought, one of my closest friends called. Instead of letting it go to voicemail and pulling the covers over my head, I thought, *This is my chance to fight back.*

When I answered, Lindsey said she was calling just to check in. I said, "I need to bring you all into some things that have been going on."

Now there was no chance of my going back into hiding. I have the kind of friends who won't leave me alone until I tell them everything. That night we got together, and I described for them the insecurities that had been growing for weeks, the nightmare, the fears of being a fraud, even the panic attack and difficulties with my family.

They wrapped me up with love and prayed and fought for me. As Lindsey dropped me off afterward, she smiled and said, "Jennie, I've never felt so close to you."

Then I called my sister and asked to get together. Over a meal, I looked in her eyes and described the hurt I felt, and she described her hurt, and we laughed at how much confusion we'd both believed. We ended up spending the day together sharing everything going on in our lives.

One by one I went to my people and did exactly what I used to be terrified to do: *I openly acknowledged that I needed them.*

I fought back against the lie that had threatened to take me down.

I am not alone.

I am not a fraud.

I have people.

YOU MIGHT BE BELIEVING the lie right now that you are alone. But what if the people you need are right around the corner?

Come close and let me tell you my hopes for us here. I **want us to trade lonely and isolated lives that experience brief bursts of connectedness for intimately connected lives that know only brief intervals of feeling alone.**

Think I'm crazy? I'm here to tell you that I'm not.

I might have momentary setbacks when the lie that I'm alone creeps back in, but I've learned not to stay there. And in recognizing that I occasionally feel lonely, in experiencing and then sharing it honestly, I've found it brings people in— because now you know you are not alone in feeling alone!

The connection you and I both long to experience? I've seen for myself that it is possible. And once I saw it, I couldn't unsee it. I couldn't not fight for this kind of life.

You'll fight for it, too, I promise.

You'll see and not be able to unsee.

Fight back the lie with me. Let's find your people.

PART

1

. . .

WE NEED
EACH OTHER

. . .

1.

THERE IS
ANOTHER WAY

■

*D*O YOU BELIEVE THAT YOU WERE BUILT FOR TRUE, RADICAL connection? Even if you're an introvert, we all are physically, emotionally, and spiritually hardwired by God for relationship. From the moment you were born until you take your last breath, deep, authentic connection is the thing your soul most craves. Not just as an occasional experience, but as a reality woven into every day of your life.

But to access this reality, you'll have to make some changes. Because something is fundamentally wrong with how we have built our lives.

We spend our evenings and weekends tucked into our little residences with our little family or our roommates or alone, staring at our little screens. We make dinner for just us and never want to trouble our neighbors for anything. We fill a small, little crevice called home with everything we could possibly need, we keep our doors locked tight, and we feel all safe and sound. But we've completely cut ourselves off from people outside our little self-protective world. We may feel comfortable and safe and independent and entertained.

But also we feel completely sad.

Nearly all of us live this way, and yet it's just not working for any of us. As I mentioned, research says that more than three in five Americans report being chronically lonely, and that number is "on the rise."[1] These stats are indicators of a grave and costly crisis. Anxiety, depression, suicidal thoughts are all on the rise. Scientists now warn that loneliness is worse for our health than obesity, smoking, lack of access to health care, and physical inactivity.[2]

So why are we letting it define our days?

Is this *living*? Is this how life is supposed to go?

Let me skip to the answer: No. It isn't supposed to be this way! You know what you were actually built for?

- Long, meaningful conversations with people who have known you for years and would donate their kidney if you needed it.
- People who drop by with pizza and paper plates unannounced because they missed you and aren't afraid to intrude.
- Regular unscheduled and unhurried time with people who feel like family, even if they aren't.
- The obvious few who scream with joy when you share your awesome news and cry with you when you share your hard stuff.
- People who show up early to help you cook and stay late to clean up.

- People who hurt you and who are hurt by you, but who choose to work through it with you instead of both of you quitting on each other.
- People who live on mission beside you, who challenge you and make you better.
- People who know they are your people, and you are theirs. People who belong to each other.

This is a book about how to find our people—the ones we'll live day in and day out with, the ones we'll risk being fully known by, the ones we'll gladly be inconvenienced by, the ones we will choose to love.

Yes, I know how complicated and exhausting making friends can be as an adult. Why didn't anyone teach us how to do this? Does it really have to be this hard? What are we missing?

I begin this journey with you aware of two things:

1. People make up the best parts of life.
2. People make up the most painful parts of life.

And I assume you picked up this book with one of those two truths more prominently fixed in your mind. So, whether you come with hopes or with fears or with both, it's okay. I suspect that if you really go all in with me, some of your fears may come true. But I also believe that your hopes will be exceeded.

It is possible to live connected—intimately connected—to other people.

———

But connection costs something, more than many are willing to pay.

If you choose to join me in this adventure of building authentic community, I promise that what you'll gain in the bargain is more than worth it, but it will require you to reconsider most everything in your life today. Specifically:

- Your daily and weekly routines.
- The way that you buy groceries.
- The new neighborhood you're considering.
- Whether or not you live near your family.
- The church you choose to be part of.
- What you do this weekend.
- And deeper still: how open you choose to be about your difficult marriage.
- And about your fight with anxiety, which is getting worse.
- And whether you'll ask the hard question of the person you love who is drinking too much.
- And if you'll forgive and fight for the people who have hurt you deeper than you could ever imagine.

Everything I'll be asking of you in our journey together requires that you risk your comfort and your routines. And yet everything in your life aches for the change I am inviting you to experience. Because I am convinced that we have been going about this all wrong.

Waiting for Connection

I still remember the day when the thought occurred to me that I didn't have any friends. I should clarify: I had plenty of friends, but those friends and I all had very full lives, which meant that our interactions were erratic—and rare. Back then, I was neck deep in parenting young kids as well as traveling a lot, speaking, and doing events with IF:Gathering, the ministry organization I lead. And while being on the road provided plenty of life-giving interactions with other women, reentry at home often came with a sting. Did any of my "friends" even realize I'd been gone? Did they know that I'd returned?

This was not my friends' fault, of course. They had obligations, commitments, relationships, and jobs of their own. In fact, they likely were asking the same questions about me: "Does Jennie know what's going on in my life? Does she even care?"

Isn't this familiar? **We're all just kind of waiting for connection to find us.** We're waiting for someone else to initiate. Someone else to be there for us. Someone else to make the plans or ask the perfectly crafted question that helps us bare our souls.

Here's what we do: We spend hours alone in our crowded, noisy, screen-lit worlds, we invest only sporadic time with acquaintances, and then we expect close friends to somehow appear in our busy lives. We think our acquaintances should just magically produce two to five BFFs. Then, we believe, our relational needs will be met.

But community is bigger than two or three friends. Community should be the way we live. Historically and practically,

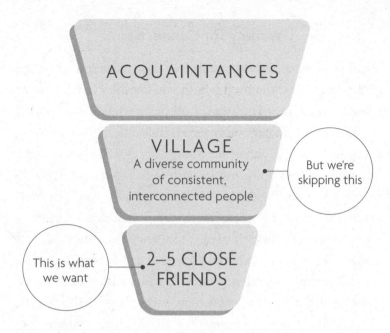

people in all countries and generations have found their friends from their larger village of interconnected people.

I've been nerding out researching this, and here's what I've learned: there are scientific studies that show how many relationships we can manage and how we socially interact with people. Basically, we can handle a network of only about 150 people. Think of your Christmas list. People you talk to at least once or twice a year. Much more than that and it falls apart!

Inside that 150 are layers of friendship that deepen with how much time you spend with a person and the degree of your relationship with them. Research suggests that we can handle only fifty people in what we will call our *acquaintances*. Within those fifty people, there are fifteen people in our *village*. And within our village, we have a capacity to make five of them our BFFs. You read that right. Only five!

Extroverts may have slightly more capacity than five, but you get the picture.

How much time you spend face to face with a person is what determines where they fit in your 150. And what pushes people deeper into our inner circles of friends?

The amount of time we spend with them.

Time.

It is our best asset when it comes to building deep community.

So, as we begin, I want you to open your mind to something more than that handful of friends you've been picturing as your goal. My dream for you, God's plan for you, is to build a culture of community in every part of your life.

My friend Curt, the neurorelational expert, said it this way: "Every newborn comes into this world looking for someone looking for her."[3] And that never quits being true.

You and I are both a little needy.

In fact, God built us this way.

And yet it's hard to need people. No, it's *terrifying* to need people, because sometimes when we acknowledge our need, we feel like there is no one who wants to take our call in the middle of the mess. Or at least that's what I believe in the moment.

Middle of a Cry

My friend I mentioned earlier, Lindsey, is the type of friend who calls me on the phone instead of texting, stops by unannounced instead of asking first, and shows up to pull me out of my robe even when I say I want to be alone.

And she calls me in the middle of a cry, when she's hurting, raw, and still confused about why she feels so sad. She lets me into the messy moments because she knows that suffering alone only makes suffering worse.

When I cry, I get it all out of my system and then maybe call a friend the next day, after I've washed my face and analyzed my situation, after I feel totally prepared to spin some optimism around the issue and top it with a slapped-on, messy, crooked bow. Because I hate how needy I actually am. I am embarrassed in my brokenness, and maybe deep down I wonder if anyone would really even want to be in the middle of that cry with me.

Which is ironic, because when Lindsey calls me crying, nothing means more to me. That phone call makes me feel needed, and who doesn't want someone to need them? So why do I keep pretending that my own need isn't real?

Obviously, I'm not writing this book because I'm an expert. I'm writing because this kind of genuine community is essential to living but we have made it an accessory.

We've replaced intrusive, real conversations with small talk, and we've substituted soul-baring, deep, connected living with texts and a night out together every once in a while, because the superficial stuff seems more manageable and less risky. But let's face it: whether we live lonely or deeply connected, life is messy. The magic of the best of relationships is the *mess,* the sitting-together-on-the-floors-of-bathrooms, hugging-and-sobbing mess.

But as I said, I'm not good at being needy. I'm needy, just not good at admitting it. And that has consistently damaged my relationships.

My tendency to hide my neediness is a painful topic for me. It always has been.

I've hurt people.

They've hurt me.

I have failed my friends. Some have forgiven me, and some have walked away. I am certain that if they knew I was writing this book, some would shake their heads and roll their eyes. *Jennie? A book on intimacy and friendship and showing up for each other over the long haul? Um . . .*

Those eye rollers would be right. While I'm doing better than I used to, I'm far from perfect in this area. And yet I'm going to keep working at it. Because the more I look into the why of our neediness and the problem of our loneliness, the more convinced I am that at our core we are made to be fully known and fully loved. Loved and known regularly and over time by family members, close friends, mentors, coworkers. **God built us for deep connection to be part of our day-in, day-out lives, not just once in a while in the presence of a paid therapist.**

It Hasn't Always Been This Way

In nearly every generation since creation began, people have lived in small communities, hunting together, cooking together, taking care of their kids together. No locks, no doors. They shared communal fires outdoors and long walks to get water, doing their best to survive day by day. People were rarely alone. They lived communally, in shared spaces, with a variety of generations present—leveraging each other's talents, sharing each other's resources, knowing each other's business, caring for each other's family members, holding each other accountable, and having each other's backs—not just to stay alive, but also in an effort to live more fulfilled . . . together.

And guess what? A lot of the world still lives this way. Hunting might have morphed into community gardens and local pubs, but most everyone who has ever lived on planet Earth has lived within a small huddle of a few dozen people, nearly always including their family but also including others, inside a radius of barely twenty miles—all their lives.

There is a foundational reason we as a generation have broken every record when it comes to how lonely we all feel.

Let me say clearly that brokenness and sin have been rampant throughout all history and all cultures. And loneliness too. Our hope in this journey isn't to re-create something old and broken but to learn from people who have approached this vital aspect of life in much healthier ways than we have. Yes, we need hope that transcends earthly relationships and connection. That is where the gospel comes in. But as one of

the first people groups on earth to live in such an individualistic way, we have much to learn from those who have chosen
connection over isolation.

TAKE ITALY. WE HAVE family there. Some people have
family in Oklahoma, but we have family in Italy. Nice, right?
A few years ago, Zac and I rented a cheap VRBO, hauled
ourselves, our four kids, and a lot of luggage onto a giant plane
to spend a week in a nontouristy little village in the middle of
Nowhere, Italy, to meet that extended family for the first time.

One afternoon, my husband and I wandered into a corner
grocery store to pick up ingredients for a dinner we'd make
later that night. We couldn't help but notice the four men
smoking and engaged in deep conversation at the counter, the
kind of conversation that looked like it might happen every
day. One of them, we'd learn, was the owner, and he, together
with the other three, seemed to be solving all the world's
problems. Our entrance interrupted their discussion, and reflexively one of the men swiveled his head toward us in a way
that seemed almost angry.

"Who are you?!" he asked.

I laughed. He wasn't impolite exactly, just surprised to see
strangers in his corner of the world. I noticed then that pretty
much every person in the market was now looking at us. We'd
evidently burst some invisible insider's bubble. The thing is,
this was a tiny town. I'm not sure exactly how many residents
lived there, but however many it was, they all knew each other.
And they all knew that strangers had shown up.

We wound up having a good conversation with several

people at the market that day, and the who-are-you guy even pointed out some Italian cookies he thought my American kids would love.

That night, while Zac and I were making dinner, I reflected on the vibe I'd picked up on in town. "Can you imagine living in a place where everyone in your whole town knows you and you know them? And where you can walk to the grocery store? And where you have to go to the grocery store at least every other day because the market—not to mention, the only market in town—carries mostly fresh food? And where that every-other-day grocery run will take you, oh, two hours or more, because you'll inevitably run into one or two or twenty-five people asking you the kinds of meaningful questions people ask when they're not strangers or even acquaintances but everyday friends?"

Cue the *Cheers* theme song now, if you are old enough to remember it.

Why don't we live in a village somewhere, I wondered, *where everyone knows our names? Where everyone would be glad we came?* I started thinking about where we lived and how we lived and whether something as simple as the lack of a local grocer might explain why I felt so lonely in sprawled-out Austin, where we lived at the time and where most of my closest friends lived a forty-five-minute drive away in traffic.

And then there's Uganda. A few years ago I traveled there with a group of people who wanted to tell the stories of South Sudanese refugees who had fled to the farmland of northern Uganda. Not only did these refugees all live together, but they worked together too. We would come to find out that they also went to church together, and that many of their children, if sponsored, attended school together.

Our little group walked up to a hut where a church service was already in progress, and the energy of the worship drew us in. People were singing and chanting and laughing. Big belly laughs. Laughs that told the world to bring it. They could take whatever life dished up. They would overcome.

Hands were raised and swaying. Babies were bouncing on the backs of women and girls alike. Feet were sliding and stomping. The place pulsed with kinetic energy, as if all fifty or sixty people in the room had merged into one.

I stood there taking it all in, the hum of this place, the elation, the cooperation, the cords of camaraderie, the sense of wild delight that covered the pain. There had to be pain, right? Of course, there was pain. So many of these people had been displaced, had lost everything—even family members. And yet to look at them was to see something more. Resolve, maybe. Or peace.

And I thought, *We don't do this very well in the place I come from.*

We don't come together in our pain.

We isolate.

We insulate.

We pretend.

We call *after* the cry.

———

And as a result, we are flat miserable.

We hole away in houses separated by fences or stay stuck in our apartments with alarms carefully set. We don't tell the whole truth of our pain because it appears that everyone else is doing just fine. They aren't hurting. In fact, they're living happy, perfect lives. We decide the problem is probably us. We hide physically because if we aren't seen, we can't be known. And if we can't be known, we can't be rejected—or worse, have our vulnerability used to hurt us even further.

We live guarded because we fear someone will use our weakness against us.

In my research, I saw a five-foot-long chart of historical people groups: who they were and where and when each group has lived. To give you a sense of our place in the overall scheme of things, the blue wedge that represents those of us living in the United States shows up only on the bottom four inches of the chart. And all I can think about as I stare at that tiny segment is how badly I wish we would embrace the approach to life that every other people group has prized. I wish we would learn to come together—showing up, speaking up, and calling each other up to a new way of life—instead of defiantly pulling ourselves apart.

We live alone, we eat alone, we run our errands alone, and we suffer alone.

And I'm sick of it.

You and I both are sick of it.

We're sick *from* it, anyway.

My Regulars

I thought of these experiences in Italy and Uganda and the hole in my life where community should be as I sat in the airport flying home—alone, once again. And I knew I wanted something to change. I wanted someone beyond my family to realize I was gone, someone to know I was coming home, and someone to process all of it with me. I decided a regular get-together with a few people was the only way for it to consistently happen. So I texted several friends I didn't yet know particularly well and explained how I was feeling and what I needed. A handful agreed to meet. Together we committed to connecting not just occasionally but regularly and intentionally.

We most often met in the evenings on my back porch, where we'd say what was true of our lives. Whenever one of us was traveling or sick, the others would get together anyway. We prioritized these times together over just about everything else. For nearly three years, we met this way. What is that, more than a hundred evenings together? At two hours a pop, we logged some serious and intimate time.

I clearly remember waiting at some gate of some airport in some town, trying to get home after speaking somewhere, and my heart would leap, knowing I would be seeing my friends the next day. Those meetups were oxygen to my connection-craving soul, gulps of fresh air I craved. We would talk about our marriages, we would talk about our kids, we would talk about our jobs, and we would talk about God. We'd laugh. We'd tear up. We'd sigh over disappointment and pain. It didn't stop with those group gatherings, either. Because we knew so much about what was happening with each other, our newfound intimacy bled into other parts of life.

We'd check in on each other.

And bring food to each other.

And shop with each other.

And listen to every small and big thing happening in our lives.

We traveled together and stuck together.

We were tight . . .

Until we were not.

One of those friends quit me. I mean, she actually looked me in the eye and said, "I don't want to be friends anymore."

I will never forget where I was sitting and how the world was spinning as she told me why she couldn't keep investing in our friendship. And as you'll see in the coming pages, this wasn't the first or last time this happened to me. Without going into details, it was completely my fault.

The point is, I lost my regulars that day. Our little team fell apart.

And yes, I still had lots of friends in Austin. But that "in Austin" part matters here. Austin is not a small town. Austin is far-flung, a hundred cities in one. If your kids aren't at my kids' schools, if your workplace isn't a block from my workplace, if your house isn't within walking distance of my house, if your favorite restaurants aren't on the same side of the lake as mine, well, then we might as well live on different planets for the number of times we'll happen to cross each other's path. I had plenty of occasional friends, people I'd see at planned times during highly scheduled events. And I loved those friends! But in terms of my real, deep, everyday friends, the women who knew my weekly comings and goings, my family's ups and downs, most of what was really going on with me, those few lunch friends were it. They were my people.

And after that one conversation with that one friend, I felt alone again.

The Best Parts Are
Also the Hardest Parts

I start with this yo-yo of a story because I think it's important that you understand how I got here. The desperate and glorious seasons of relationships in my life represent what is true for you and me both:

Outside of Jesus, relationships are the greatest gifts we have on earth and simultaneously the most difficult part of being alive.

————

There are seasons when it feels like our relational cup is over-flowing and seasons when we wonder if anyone even knows we are alive.

Maybe you're a pastor's wife who knows the whole church but never really feels known.

Or you're single and just moved to a new town for a job and have to completely start over, alone.

Or you live alone and worry who would take care of your dog if you had to go to the hospital for some reason.

Or you have a lot of people who you consider friends, but you don't feel a deep connection with anyone.

Or you've tried three small groups and still haven't found the right fit.

Or you had the best of friends, but life happened and you drifted apart.

Or maybe you feel like you have absolutely no one and don't even know where to begin.

Whatever situation has left you feeling detached and adrift, I'm about to throw you a life preserver.

2.

THE CONNECTION
WE CRAVE

■

A VILLAGE: IT'S A STATE OF BEING WE ALL DESIRE. HOW DO I KNOW this? Because whenever I have a stressful day, guess what I turn on at the end of it?

The television show *Friends*.

Why did we love that show so much? The coffee-shop second home, the never-locked doors, the communal living, the unique personalities that stuck it out with one another no matter what. For a decade, those six friends did everything together. They laughed and cried and cheered and sighed— adulting, arm in arm. They were each other's constant. They were each other's home, and when we watched them, we felt like they were our friends, like their home was our home too. And while those six had been many not-so-great things along the way—neurotic and needy, offendable and obsessed, ridiculous and self-righteous, possessive and downright jerks—the one thing they'd never been was alone.

Nothing felt more wrong to me than the last episode of the series. Monica and Chandler brought their adopted twin babies into the world and then moved a world away. Or that's how it seemed, anyway. Right when they would need their friends the most, they settled for a swing set and a yard. I was appalled.

And yet so many of us make the very same trade.

We move to cool cities. We move for higher-paying jobs. We choose colleges for their reputation. We choose churches for the best preaching. We hunt for our dream home in the "right" neighborhoods. We shape our lives around a set of values that were handed to us from our terribly independent, success-driven culture.

But are we happy?

Why We Crave Deep, Intimate Relationship

A few years ago, I went home to see my parents for the weekend and got together with some friends from childhood days. Nearly every one of my close friends from junior high and high school still live in the same community where we grew up. These girls became adults, moved out of their parents' homes, went to college, got married, and then bought homes of their own just blocks from where their parents still live. When I go back to visit, it's like rewinding to me, age seventeen. The streets are the same. The trees, while bigger, are the same. The landmarks are the same. My friends are exactly the same.

Anyway, that weekend, after three or four hours of sitting around the table eating, laughing, commiserating, and reliving a hundred hilarious memories, we started vision casting about the retirement house on the beach we will one day share after our husbands are gone. We were joking (kind of), but the idea of deep-down communal living made my heart sing, and as much as I love my family, there is something about the vision of dear friends cooking together and sharing the daily mundane that sounds pretty perfect to me.

If you are an introvert, I worry that you're about to put down this book. I realize that I am hardwired for relational connectivity more than most people, but please hear me out:

Even if a house full of friends isn't your dream come true, you were built by God for deep relationships.

In fact, God existed in relationship with Himself before any of us were here. It's called the Trinity. God is one, and God is three. (If you've never heard this before, don't worry. It hurts my brain still, and I've been to seminary.) The key point is this: for all eternity, God has existed in relationship—as Father, Spirit, and Son (Jesus).[1]

Scripture says that the Son exists to glorify the Father, and that the Father exists to glorify the Son. It says that the Spirit exists to glorify them both. What that means is that they help each other, they promote each other, they serve each other, and they love each other. What's more, this exchange has been going on for all eternity.[2]

It means that our God has been relational forever. It means that He created us *out of* relationship *for* relationship—and not a relationship that is surface level or self-seeking. No, the relationship He has in mind for us is . . .

> sacrificial,
>> intimate,
>>> moment-by-moment connection.

Author and pastor Tim Keller said,

> The life of the Trinity is characterized not by self-centeredness but by mutually self-giving love. When we delight and serve someone else, we enter into a dynamic orbit around him or her, we center on the interests and desires of the other. That creates a dance, particularly if there are three persons, each of whom moves around the other two.[3]

Beautiful.

Relational. It's who we are, because it's who God is.

We were made in the image of God, who *is* relationship. This means our longing for healthy, mutually submissive, supportive, interdependent relationships isn't simply us craving something good for us, like vegetables or vitamins; we are craving the fundamental reason we were created. **We weren't just built *for* community; we were built because of it.** Woven into the fiber of our souls is a pattern for experiencing intimate relationship with God and then expressing that love in our families and communities and churches.

But here is where we go wrong. We look to people to complete and fill what only God was meant to fill. This is the primary reason we all are so unhappy with each other. We have put our hope in imperfect people. But that hope can successfully be answered only in God Himself. Eternity was set in our hearts, Ecclesiastes 3:11 says, which means only a relationship with an eternal God can fill our hearts.

Consider what you're aiming your hope toward. Who is in the center of your affections? Who is in the center of your identity? We all have a choice. The answer will determine whether you live fulfilled or repeatedly disappointed.

If God is in the center of our relational circle, we will be fulfilled, and out of that fulfillment we can bless others. But if people are in the center of our relational circle, we end up pulling on others to meet needs that they can't ever fully meet.

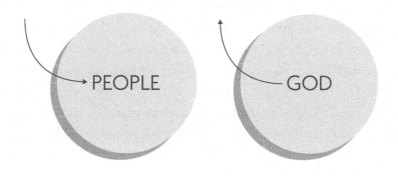

Jesus said it clearest. When asked to name the greatest commandment, He said all the commandments could be boiled down to this: "Love the Lord your God with all your heart and with all your soul and with all your mind. This is the great and first commandment. And a second is like it: You shall love your neighbor as yourself."[4]

When you have God in the right place, at the center of

your affections, you will more likely get people right. So, yes, that relationship comes first, but that relationship is meant to send us into loving others.

God Desires Community for Us

Throughout Scripture we see that God keeps building communities. In the Old Testament He starts with a family. That family becomes a people group. That people group grows into the nation of Israel. Throughout the New Testament you see God's heart for the local church.

This is the way God moves throughout history. Family, community, a nation, and local church that reaches the world. God loves us to be together. God loves us to be on mission together. God loves us to worship Him together. Jesus said, "For where two or three are gathered in my name, there am I among them."[5] We know that our togetherness matters to God.

The Bible was penned in the context of people daily living interconnected lives. The teachings of Scripture to Israel and to the Church assume people belonging to and depending on a group. In fact throughout most of the Bible, when it says "you," the original Hebrew and Greek languages nearly always indicate a plural form: you all (or y'all, depending on how godly y'all are).

The Bible doesn't speak to individuals. It's written for people living out their faith together!

And this all matters so much because . . .

We make each other better. "As iron sharpens iron, so one person sharpens another."[6]

We remind each other of God and His plans for us. "That you and I may be mutually encouraged by each other's faith."[7]

We fight for each other to not be distracted by sin. "But exhort one another every day, as long as it is called 'today,' that none of you may be hardened by the deceitfulness of sin."[8]

We complete each other. "As it is, there are many parts, but one body."[9]

We need each other to live out the purposes of God. "Each member belongs to all the others. We have different gifts."[10]

How arrogant are we to think that even though the God of the universe exists in community, our little fragile finite selves can survive without it? No, there is a beautiful God-built plan for having our souls be full, satisfied.

If this plan is so good for us, why don't we just prioritize this plan, fight for this plan, and make this plan unfold every day of our lives?

Two words:

the enemy.

The Enemy Hates Community

Think about it: if God is relationship and He created us for relationship, then guess who hates it?

I mean, if deep, loving, intimate connection is God's goal, then the enemy might hate nothing more than for you and me to enjoy deep, loving, intimate connection! And that's why this isn't a feel-good book about how to make friends. This is a depiction of war, a description of two distinct sides, and a reminder that *everything* is at stake.

No wonder it feels like every aspect of our lives is stacked against our connection to other people.

It is.

That enemy seeks to destroy this good thing God created on the earth out of His love. **The enemy wants to divide us.** Rather than fighting for each other, he wants to see us fighting against each other. He wants to prevent the glory of God from shining through this city on a hill, a gathering of believers who are set apart for the purpose of displaying God to the world.

We are called to be a community of people, on a mission, delighting in God, delighting in each other, redeemed and reconciling the world, bringing them and inviting them into this family. *This* is the ultimate purpose of community.

Yes, it is to encourage you.

———

Yes, it is to comfort you.

Yes, it is to fight for you.

But ultimately community is meant to open the doors wide to every person on earth and invite them into a family that exists forever with God.

Yes, a life of connection is for your thriving, but this is also for eternity.

We must understand the war we're in. We must understand that the enemy is subtle and sneaky and seeks to destroy you by destroying your relationships. We have no better defensive weapon than having the people who love God rally around us, fight for us, and fight with us.

Maybe you don't believe in God or in Jesus. If so, please know how glad I am that you're here and how deeply I wish we could meet. And I hope you encounter in these pages a God who built you, loves you, and has a plan for you to live with joy and connection to Him and to others.

We all crave a collective belonging. Because God built us for it.

And what should be true of us who love Jesus and follow Him is that, because we have found our identity in Him, we enter human relationships without lists of expectations and neediness. **Christ followers enter human relationships full of hope and full of confidence to love others, regardless of the treatment they receive in return.**

Oh, I am fully aware this is not our reputation. And I am genuinely sorry for the ways that Christians may have caused harm to you or to people you love. (Being Christian means we have been freed from the slavery of sin but not from the desire of it.)

Truly, no one has taught me more about friendship than Jesus, and I hope as we journey together you will see how brilliant and full of life-giving grace He is. Jesus is the best imaginable friend. And He helps us become the same.

How Did We Get Here?

As I've already mentioned, nearly every generation that has ever lived has experienced a village existence. Between Jesus's days here on earth and the Reformation fifteen hundred years later, a custom practiced the world over was that for every twenty-five young people in a given place, a school would be established.[11] In Jesus's world, for example, it was actually *illegal* for a family to live somewhere without a school close by, and so for every twenty-five boys, a teacher would be appointed.

Families whose children went to school together also worshipped together, meeting first in homes and then in appointed buildings as the community grew. Educational life and social life and religious life and vocational life and family life all bled together.

Bottom line, people were in each other's business.

But that has all radically changed. Our priorities no longer center on "we" but on "me."

Individualism as we know it has long, deep roots that date centuries back.

France saw individualism break forth in the massive anarchy called the French Revolution.

Closer to home, the Revolutionary War against Britain by the United States was all about

> Freedom.
> > Independence.
> > > Individual rights.

I mean, come on. One of our first acts as Americans was to draft a document called the Declaration of Independence.

"Independence!" was our battle cry.

Independent became our core identity.

Hey, I am terribly grateful America exists, and I don't for one minute take for granted the freedoms we enjoy. But that independent spirit has a dark side. **For the past 250 years, we have been declaring our independence with increasing pitch and volume, with greater and greater insistence that we can handle life on our own.**

From settlers spreading out and building a life for their families in this vast country to the Industrial Revolution in the late 1700s that forced small villages of farmers and their families to fence their properties and become factory workers in big cities,[12] we have been on a downward spiral, away from community.

Loneliness first began to show up in a significant way at the rise of the Industrial Revolution.[13] When factories automated everything, people's lives became easier and more self-reliant. But efficiency came at a great cost; namely, we didn't need each other all the time.

I should mention here that a full 80 percent of the world's population still exists in the context of small, community-based groups—villages, you might call them—where what's mine is always ours.[14] But for those of us here in the West, life doesn't look like that.

Likely springing from the Enlightenment's focus on individualism, the self-help movement of the late twentieth century set personal happiness as the ultimate prize.[15] And then came the birth of social media in 1997, which rewards with "likes" personal-branding continuity and snarky one-upmanship.

Independence has become the chief value in this country.

We are brainwashed that "being a self-made woman" (or man), "making our own way," and striving for "personal achievement" are the goals of our brief, beautiful lives. For generations now, we have taken the bait, believing that siloed, individualistic, pull-yourself-up-by-your-bootstraps living will somehow satisfy in the end.

And yet the book I base my life on, as well as the God who built us, starts the whole, big story with these two lines:

"Let us create man in our image."

"It is not good for man to be alone."

And deep down inside, we know this to be true.

We are meant to live in community, moment by moment, breath by breath. Not once a week or once a month at a night out with friends or during lunch after emerging from an isolated cubical.

———

But every moment, every day, for the entirety of our lives.

So how the heck are we supposed to fight terrifying stats of loneliness, the devil and his plan to sabotage connection, and the fundamental way that society is set up, and instead build what God cares most about?

It's going to take a village. You know the saying, "It takes a village to raise a child." Well, it takes a village to create a full and thriving life for us adults too.

But this village living will not happen by accident.

We'll have to build a new life.

3.

A VISION FOR
SOMETHING MORE

■

*I*N 2017, AFTER LIVING FOR MORE THAN A DECADE IN THE SAME place, my family decided to move to Dallas, Texas. "After eleven years in a city we love," I wrote in a post online, "we are moving from Austin, Texas, to Dallas. . . . In the last week, doors closed with schooling for our youngest two, who have learning differences. So, faced with spreading our family all over the city of Austin in three different schools, we chose instead to pull everyone in close and to move near family."

The post was all true. But it was also incomplete. Yes, the school issue had become a real dilemma. But it also just felt like the sprawling nature of Austin was not working for us anymore. We never saw some of our most beloved friends, and our extended family lived too far away for us to get together on a regular basis. Even with all the amazing people we loved in Austin, we still felt lonely. Would a move help?

When I told one of my family members about our plans, she both celebrated our decision and forecast the doom I feared: "I think your kids will be fine, Jennie. I just worry about you. I'm afraid you'll be lonely starting over in such a big city."

I swallowed hard and reupped my commitment to this plan. Zac's job and my organization could move. And even if they couldn't, we were craving a new way to live that transcended our jobs and house size. We were ready to see if we could build a life around people.

Now, let me calm your fears: What we are about to discuss here will not necessitate a move for you. So don't go scrolling Zillow just yet. But something about our family's experience in starting over from scratch clarified for me was what it takes to build this kind of deeply entrenched community—wherever you may be.

When my husband and kids and I relocated two hundred miles to the north, the move represented the first family-wide upheaval in over a decade. For years, we'd been humming along, making our way through the young-children ages and stages and goings-on of life that everyone knows and loves. We had established rhythms with church, school, sports activities, and all the usual aspects of home and family maintenance. We had our places to shop and hang out. Life was a little isolated but predictable.

And then, the move.

With the exception of Zac's family and a few friends from previous seasons of life spread across the metroplex, the six of us were starting over. With four anxious kids and my family members' gloomy forecast beating back my usual optimism, the stakes seemed ridiculously high.

On the big day, having unintentionally beat the movers by four hours, Zac pulled into our new driveway and exhaled. Was it relief he was feeling, or frustration? I didn't know, and I'm not sure I cared. I was more concerned about the panic attack building inside me.

I walked through the front door of this place that was supposed to be home. As empty as the rooms felt, the city felt emptier. We were lost here.

Not only did I not know where to buy groceries or get a haircut, but I had four kids who each needed friends, doctors, tutors, mentors, people to call their own. I didn't know where to turn for help. The ache of needing everything and knowing next to no one intensified. I felt sure that we could settle our home in a few days. But would our souls ever settle again?

"Shoot, I forgot to get rug pads!" I snapped at Zac.

"What?" he said, distracted by the loads needing to be brought in from the car.

"The rug pads!" I was on the verge of tears. The movers would soon be arriving, ready to dump our stuff, and if I could just get those stupid rug pads down first, then we could start to build our life here. But I'd forgotten them. It was nothing, and it was everything. I was spinning.

Zac saw panic flash in my eyes. "I'll find some pads," he whispered, as he slipped by.

In the days preceding the move, I'd had the presence of mind to call the college pastor at the church we'd soon be joining. Did he know of a kind, responsible young woman who could be our babysitter? Cooper, our youngest, was nine at the time, and while many nine-year-olds require little supervision, Cooper's RPMs have always run high. Given how full my hands would be with the move, the transition of IF:Gathering to a new town, the general nuttiness of establishing a new six-person household, and my own emotional tailspins, I figured a sure, steady presence would be a gift to Cooper—and to me.

Two hours after the trip up I-35, we'd unloaded the car and I was sitting on the dining room floor of our empty new house, crying embarrassing crocodile tears in front of the young and lovely Caroline Parker, who probably wondered what on earth she'd gotten herself into.

"I need help," I admitted, as if it weren't obvious.

Caroline sat there totally expressionless, earning my confidence with her quiet, nonjudging presence. "I'm not easily stressed out," she said to me.

I told her I thought we'd get along just fine.

In the middle of my desperation, God had dropped into my life a college-aged babysitter who would go on to love my kids, fold dozens of loads of laundry for me, work at IF:Gathering, become part of our family, and to this day be one of my safest coworkers and friends in this city.

Caroline Parker taught me in short order that my little village here was going to (1) come because of my neediness and desperation, not in spite of it, and (2) be built in unexpected ways and with unexpected people.

More Than Just a
Few Good Friends

Why is it that the most frequent question I am asked online is "How do I make friends?" With all the problems we are facing as a society, you might assume that I am exaggerating, but ask my team and they'll confirm: this is *the* question.

It sounds like something first graders would ask, you know? When my kids were that age, they would show up at school and have to make new friends, a skill they obviously didn't yet have. But no, this is something sixty-year-olds are asking, twenty-five-year-olds are asking, young moms are asking. And I get it, because the art of making and keeping friends was never really spelled out for most of us.

We learned how to read and write and name the planets, dress ourselves, get a job, and even have sex, but no one ever really sat down and taught us how to make a friend or how to be a friend.

Is it possible that we (all of us, I mean) are asking the wrong question? Making friends, yes, that's a concern—as is keeping them. **But what if that intimate circle we're craving is actually found in the wider network of the village that we've been missing?**

We wait for those perfect few friends to come along, and then we look for them to play so many roles in our lives. We look to them to be *everything* to us. What if the power of a little team of friends is that each one brings different things to your life?

I have fun friends who always make a plan and always

make me laugh. I have wise friends who give me advice and call me out. I have encouraging friends who cheer me on and tell me what I'm doing well. I have challenging friends who disrupt my thinking and push back against assumptions I have made or push me to take greater risks.

If I expected one or two people to fill all those roles, no one would ever hit the mark. Also true: if I didn't appreciate the unique roles my friends play in my life, I might be mad that my "challenger" friend doesn't encourage me more, or my "wise" friend isn't fun all the time.

If I start to see that God has put different people in my life to bless me in different ways, then I can both embrace who they are and rest in what I bring to those relationships. These words from C. S. Lewis, written after losing a dear friend he shared with J. R. R. (Ronald) Tolkien, helped me see how my different friends and their unique value in my life are irreplaceable.

> In each of my friends there is something that only some other friend can fully bring out. By myself I am not large enough to call the whole man into activity; I want other lights than my own to show all his facets. Now that Charles is dead, I shall never again see Ronald's reaction to a specifically [Charles] joke. Far from having more of Ronald, having him "to myself" now that Charles is away, I have less of Ronald.[1]

Maybe the question we are really asking behind the question of "How do I make friends?" is this: "How can I belong to an intimate community of people?"

Needing Each Other Is
Not Weakness but Strength

As I sat on my dining room floor in our new home in Dallas, which, as you'll recall, had no furniture yet, crying in front of my new babysitter, Caroline, while feeling alone and afraid, a clear memory came to mind.

I pictured myself back in Rwanda, where Zac and I traveled to meet our new son, Cooper. It was late spring 2011, and I was in the passenger seat of a tiny ramshackle van, staring out the window as the driver slowly bumped us along a rutted road. Every few feet, I'd see another mass of women, all different ages walking together, water jugs balanced atop their heads, making their way back to their homes. I couldn't understand what they were saying, but their countenance transcended language. They were talking. Laughing. Filling in blanks for each other. Loving each other well. They were tight. They all were tight. This wasn't a series of cliques; this was a community. A village. An entire town that knew everything about everyone—and was better off for it, no doubt.

"You're giving your son such a better life," people in this country would say after I returned home with Cooper's hand in mine. But I knew the truth. Yes, he would have a family and his needs would be met, but we had also stripped him of a vibrant, interdependent culture to bring him to the hyperindividualized U.S. of A. I was transplanting Cooper to the land of fast loneliness, praying that the four years he had in Rwanda would keep him tethered to Africa's relationally saner way of life and committed to bring him back as often as we could afford.

"You do everything alone in America," our good friend in Rwanda, Pastor Charles Mugisha, always reminds me. "We [Rwandans] do everything together."

For better or worse, in the traditional village structure, the people all know your name.

More sobering still: they all know your pain.

But time and again, they throw in to help you survive, to help you get through this thing called life.

Somewhere in the transition from hunting and gathering and cooking together to having our groceries delivered to our doorstep or the back of our car, we stopped needing each other. We don't need each other to survive anymore. We don't even need to borrow an egg.

Or do we?

Professor and author Brené Brown famously told the story of a group of women in a remote village in Africa who spent their late afternoons at the river's edge, washing their families' clothes by hand.[2] There in the sunlight, they would swap stories. They would ask questions. They would check in with each other. Most days, they would laugh so hard that they'd cry.

These women were stuck in the throes of poverty, but you wouldn't know it, aside from the tattered clothing and the obvious detail that they were forced to wash clothes in mucky waters.

Well, sometime later, the entire village experienced a massive shift in its resourcefulness, after residents learned to plant and harvest crops. They could sell fruits and vegetables in a larger town nearby. With their new income, they could afford uniforms and send their kids to school. They could upgrade their modest huts to substantial, permanent structures. They could wire their lives with electricity. They could dig wells and finally have clean water. They could even buy a few modern conveniences, like cell phones, toaster ovens—and washing machines.

Interestingly, once nearly every home in the village had its own washing machine, the prevalence of depression among the moms in that region rose sharply. What was going on here? The village was thriving, right? Look at all the stuff they had!

The explanation may not be obvious to you and me, but it is to people like Pastor Mugisha, who was raised in a family of refugees following the Rwandan genocide of 1994. After coming to the States for the first time, he made this observation to me:

"The more resources a person gets, the more walls he or she puts up. And the more lonely they become."

The Beginning and the End

Let's step back for just a minute to gain perspective. I like to start with the end in mind. If I know the goal, then I can build an effective strategy to reach it.

So let's go all the way to the very end, to heaven, where we will be surrounded by people who love God, people from every nation, every tribe.[3] We will be together forever, with no more

death, division, comparison, fighting—no sin. Not just singing in some heavenly choir but **living, working, relating, eating, loving, worshipping, enjoying God forever with a diverse
group of people we recognize and who recognize us—forever.**

That's the future, where we are headed.

Now, let's look back to the beginning to see how we got to
where we are right now.

WE CAN'T START ANY further back than Genesis 1:1: "In
the beginning, God."

As I've mentioned, God existed in community and created
us out of His love. Genesis 2:18 says that after God had created one person on the earth, Adam, He said, "It is not good
for the man to be alone" (NIV).

So God created Eve, and He gave Adam and Eve everything they needed to thrive, to grow, and to live together on
the earth. The first two humans lived together with God in
the garden. They were naked and unashamed. No shame before each other, and no shame before God. Just free, beautiful
love and the safety of authentic relationship. They shared the
goal of caring for creation. They were given a boundary (just
one). And they had all the time in the world to enjoy God,
His creation, and each other.

When I slow down and really consider what life looked
like back in the Garden of Eden, I see five realities:

1. **Proximity.** They enjoyed physical closeness to
    each other and God.

2. **Transparency.** They were naked and unashamed,
    fully known and fully loved.
3. **Accountability.** They lived under submission to
    God and to each other.
4. **Shared Purpose.** They were given a clear calling
    to care for creation.
5. **Consistency.** They couldn't quit each other. They
    needed each other and shared everything
    together.

These five "tastes of heaven" provide the framework for
how we build healthy community in our own lives today. God
established a perfect community that we can work to reclaim
here and now.

The Repercussions
of Independence

I say "work to reclaim" because that's about all that we can
hope for in our present reality. Because Adam and Eve wanted
independence more than connection and they bucked God's
authority, shame entered their relationship, they forfeited
close proximity with their Creator, they corrupted their God-
given purpose, and time began to count down to a grave. Sin
entered the world.

Since the beginning of time, we've fought hard for the independence we think we want—not just Adam and Eve, or
you and me, or the three-in-five people who admit to being
lonely pretty much all the time[4]—but rather every human
who has ever lived.

There is no one righteous, not even one;
there is no one who understands;
there is no one who seeks God.
All have turned away.[5]

It's the story of humankind. We see the repercussions of that independence everywhere. But nowhere is it shown more clearly than in our human relationships.

We all hurt others. We all sin. We all push people away. We all are guilty.

Nothing in my relational life has helped me more than coming to terms with these simple truths:

You will disappoint me. I will disappoint you. God will never disappoint us.

Accepting this shifts our expectations from people to God. And He can handle our expectations.

4.

FINDING YOUR
PEOPLE

■

*A*FTER ZAC AND I LANDED IN DALLAS, WE WASTED NO TIME IN finding a church our family could call home. With four kids who were experiencing varying levels of anxiety about the restart, not to mention my own tailspin, we needed to act fast. We did exactly zero church shopping, choosing to simply return to the church we'd attended twelve years prior, when we had briefly lived in Dallas to attend seminary.

Next, when I learned that my camp counselor from twenty-five years earlier happened to be living in the same town and attending the same church, I swallowed my embarrassment over being essentially friendless and asked if she'd be my friend.

To be fair, it didn't exactly go like that. But that's precisely how it felt. Michelle is only three or four years older than I am, but given our bond when I was a teenager, I took the risk of initiating a conversation. When she showed up at the coffee shop with minimal makeup and wearing a plain T-shirt and workout shorts, I knew we could be good friends. This was Dallas, where standard dress for the grocery store rivals my Austin wedding attire.

I cannot overstate how monumental this singular decision was, in the overall course of things. You may not believe me when I tell you this, but one simple phone call, one seemingly inconsequential text, can shift your course entirely. It can set into motion a cascade of events. As it turned out, Michelle was in the process of joining a small group at our now-mutual church. "You know about the small groups?" she said to me, her eyes revealing some of the doubt she obviously carried.

"What about them?" I said, matching her tone of reservation.

"You join them for life," Michelle said. Our church, as I would soon discover, takes community very, very seriously.

As in, tell-the-truth-about-your-struggles seriously.

As in, tell-the-*whole*-truth-about-your-struggles seriously.

As in, disclose-the-details-of-your-finances-with-each-other seriously.

Not kidding, even a little. In these community groups, *everything* is fair game.

So, anyway, in the midst of giving me a little primer on our church's views on community groups, Michelle blurted out, "You and Zac should join ours!"

Uh. No.

"No, thank you." I mean, *Thank you!* And yet, *no.*

I wanted friends, but I also wanted some time to be sure that we were throwing in with the right people. Coming off some friendship failures in Austin, the mere mention of life-long commitment made me reflexively step back. Since then,

I've learned that plenty of small groups don't quite make it the proposed four or more decades. But I felt the pressure.

I tend to be gregarious in social situations and come off extremely extroverted, engaged, and fun, but raise the stakes and dive into how life *really* is going, and man, do my walls go up fast. And now a bunch of perfect strangers were supposed to have access to my deepest thoughts? My desires? My spending patterns? My use of time? Yikes.

I should mention here that that conversation happened almost four years ago, and Zac and I risked it and jumped in with that small group of people and still are together today. And those friends we did not intentionally choose? They are some of the closest friends that we have.

Don't get me wrong: at many turns along the way, things between people in that group and us have been incredibly difficult. Especially at first, it was awkward. As in, *awkward*.

Had I not been so desperate to find my people, I probably would have bailed. Thankfully I stayed. Thankfully, when the invitation came to engage in candid, authentic, long-term community, I whispered an earnest *yes*. **That one yes has changed everything.**

Do You Want This?

Let me assure you that today I have my village. Since that coffee date, a handful of other friends have come into my life too. You'll hear more as we go. My network of people is diverse and intrusive, and they hold me up and together. I love them, and they are in and out of my life most every minute of every day. And I want this for you, if you don't already have it. More important, God wants this for you.

My suspicion? You want this too.

I think that's why you are here. I am guessing you are here because you're sick of the ache. I am guessing people have hurt you and you hope there is another way to do this. I am guessing you are looking for a vision and for tools to help you build healthier relationships. And I imagine that by this point in the book, you might feel a little afraid. You are afraid that this book won't provide any relief for your deepest longings and hopes and dreams, and that possibly our whole system is just universally broken.

If that's you, then please hear me: because our current world has been built on such rampant independence . . .

it will take deliberate intention to return to the kinds of relationships that God had in mind for us to enjoy.

But we *can* return.

At this point you also may be saying, "Sounds great! I would love to find my people, but I've tried, and for the most part, people are just incredibly toxic and draining. Are you sure this is a good idea?"

I hear you.

Choosing our people isn't as simple as finding people to wash clothes by the river with or take walks with; we need these friends to be healthy. Not perfect, but also not toxic—is that too much to ask?

Our Model for a Life of Community

I mentioned earlier that Jesus has taught me more about friendship than anyone else. Let me tell you why I like Him so much.

I've always related to the words of Psalm 8:4: "[God,] *what is man that you are mindful of him?*" (emphasis added). I understand the question. If there is a God who set all this in motion (and there is!), and if He has existed forever, started this big, beautiful earth spinning, created every human being, and placed breath in each of our lungs, then how can it be that that God concerns Himself with sinful, broken us? Further, if sinful people refuse to turn toward that God, acknowledge that God, love that God, and devote themselves mind, body, and spirit to that God, then who in a right mind could blame Him for smiting them all? Why *wouldn't* He send a big fat meteor and just take out the globe?

Ephesians 2 tells us that we—you and I and everyone ever to live—were dead in our trespasses and sins, and that we were children of wrath, meaning that we deserved for God to send that meteor our way. "But God, being rich in mercy, because of the great love with which he loved us, even when we were dead in our trespasses, made us alive together with Christ."[1]

But God.

> Through Christ.
> Because of love.
> Rescued us.
> Made us alive.

———

Let me tell you how these few phrases change everything.

Jesus rescuing us from our sin and giving us a way out changes not only our eternal future with Him, but it also empowers us to love like Him here. "All this is from God, who through Christ reconciled us to himself and gave us the ministry of reconciliation."[2]

You and I are to give that reconciliation and hope away to living, breathing, broken, longing people. God purposefully set you in your place and in your time to love people in such a way that they will feel their way toward Him and find Him.[3]

Jesus not only provides the means to live a full, thriving life with each other and with Father God, He also modeled how it would look! He chose to come to earth not only to die for our sins but to show us how to live as children of God.

So here are just a few things you need to know about when God came to earth:

- Jesus was born into an earthly family, with a mom and a dad and siblings.
- He grew up in a neighborhood with family friends and other kids.
- He learned a trade—carpentry—from his dad.
- He experienced temptation but never sinned.
- He laughed and learned and sang and grew up in the context of a village.
- He found His people in unexpected places, not universities or temples. His people were prosti-

tutes, uneducated fishermen, hated tax collectors, children, mothers-in-law. They were often, by any onlooker's estimation, the wrong ethnicity, the wrong gender, the wrong age, the wrong status, the wrong personality type, the wrong people.

Jesus's people were all wrong—except that they were *willing*. And they were *wanting*. And they were all in.

That seems to be the only universally clear marker of the small group of people Jesus chose to spend His time with. They were willing. They were wanting. They were *all in*.

You may recall that Jesus made a habit of pushing away crowds and eating with His few. He pushed the crowds away and chose twelve. Within that twelve, there were three He spent the most time with. They were His closest people. The ones He confided in the most. The short version? It's okay to be selective as we go forward. You will need to be.

Jesus and His people would go on to help a lot of people "feel their way" toward God. What began in a village with a tight group of people would reach generations and the ends of the earth. This is the endgame of community: **we find our people, and together we build safe, beautiful outposts that offer the love of God.**

Village-sized community works because it's what we were built to handle—you know, five to fifty people, max. The internet is not your village. Every problem you hear about in the news is not yours to solve. We are exhausted from trying. We need to rebuild our infrastructure with healthy villages and commit to being healthy participants in the villages that we build. There will be times it doesn't feel like the happier, easier way. We need a deep conviction in our bones to stick with it and live not lonely.

You and I both desire deep connection. We want someone to know our deepest, darkest secrets and to love us anyway. But that type of community doesn't come naturally. We have to look for it and then fight to protect it once we have it.

This Won't Be Perfect

A note of clarification, as we begin. You and I both are unhealthy people. Hopefully not completely unhealthy, but somewhat unhealthy for sure. Everyone has pockets of sin in their lives, and you and I are no different. The point? You will never find the perfect people to do life with you, because those people don't exist. **You will always be doing community with sinners.**

With that in mind, we approach this work with humility. A *lot* of humility. At the same time, we are told throughout Scripture to use discernment about the people we do life with.

Who are we looking for?

In the "village" that Zac and I have built, there are two categories of people I spend my time with:

People who need me.

People I need.

People who need me may not have much to offer in return, but what they can give me isn't the point. I am there to love them, serve them, and encourage them—that's it.

Remember the culture of community I talked about in chapter 1? Our lives should be built around layers of increasingly meaningful friendships, from acquaintances, to our village, to our inner circle. Think of it this way:

Who's Your Inner Circle?

In the coming chapters we will walk through patterns of living that will help you find your people and deepen your relationships with those people. But before we run headlong into this work, it's important to talk about what you are looking for.

First, remember that your inner circle can't be huge—no more than five people. Your village might be made up of coworkers, Sunday school teachers, kids' friends' parents, your dorm floor, and so on. We live busy lives and don't have the margin to "do life" in any sort of meaningful way with a group fifty people strong. If you have fifty people in your life, we would call those people *acquaintances*. Your inner circle is made up of the people who are keeping tabs on you day by day and who know the state of your heart. These are the people you're going to call to tell about a fight you had with your husband or a difficulty at work or a fear or sin you've been battling.

My inner circle is made of a handful of people who see me and know me and who are willing to be seen and known by me. They're imperfect, admittedly. But they're determined to grow and become more like Christ, and that was the qualifier for me. We aren't the same age, and we don't approach all issues the same way, but we share a common pursuit of God. I love God more because of them. And hopefully they would say the same of me.

You might be thinking, *Are you saying my friends all need to be friends with each other?* No. They're probably coming from different parts of your life. We're not talking about five people who all know each other. I may be one of your five, but your other four may not be part of my five. Your people might come from different groups.

So what should you look for?

Availability. Look for people who say yes and show up even with kids in tow, even with a messy house, even before they've had a chance to shower.

Humility. Look for people willing to say hard things and receive hard things. We need humility to work things out, and growth happens in all our lives only if we aren't so arrogant that we think we don't need to change or that the problem is someone else.

Transparency. We'll talk more about this later, but for now, look for someone who refuses to hide, people who will say what's really going on in their lives. Watch for the ones who will articulate the hard, messy truth rather than a sanitized version that goes down a little easier.

Obviously, healthy friendships will inevitably have conflict, but in my experience these three qualities in a relationship help sinners stay together over time.

I should mention here that the apostle Paul wasn't afraid to caution us against aligning with unhealthy people. Paul talked about people we should avoid, those who live as if "their god is their belly, and they glory in their shame."[4] In other words, people who are comfortable in their sin, people who mistakenly believe that they don't need to change—those should not be the ones who make up your inner circle.

If you are running with people like this, you will get complacent fast. Our flesh loves to not be bothered about its sin. Run—don't walk—away from toxic people who will lead you into sin and away from God. Instead, **choose friends who will fight for you, friends who will fight alongside you, and friends who are as committed as you are to fighting against the dark.**

Pray for this.

Ask God right now for these people.

———

Even if you haven't prayed in a long time, right now close your eyes and form words begging Him to help you find people to live this way with. He can bring these people to you in unexpected ways. Believe that He can and that He wants to bless you with people to do this difficult life with.

And pray to become this.

We can't have what we aren't willing to become.

God's idea of community is deep, intentional, day-in and day-out connection, loving at all times, bearing with one another, sticking closer than siblings, naming every sin, running our races together, encouraging each other as long as it is called today.[5]

The reality of His intentional design is made clear not only in God's Word but in scientifically observable fact.

For several years now, smart people have been researching why people who live in the happiest places on earth—called Blue Zones—experience a much better quality of life, a much longer quantity of life, and greater health overall.[6] Is it their diet? Is it their position relative to the equator? Is it their exercise regimen? Why are people who live in these specific places—Okinawa, Japan; Sardinia, Italy; Nicoya, Costa Rica; Ikaria, Greece; and Loma Linda, California—doing so much better than the rest of us? What's the one thing we all should do?

As it turns out, the reason those villagers with washing machines became depressed all those years ago, and the reason inhabitants of the happiest places on earth thrive so distinctively today, is the same: *camaraderie.*

We're not meant to go through our days alone.

We're not meant to learn alone.
Or to work alone.
Or to do chores alone.
Or to relax alone.
Or to celebrate alone.
Or to cry alone.
Or to make decisions alone.

The Experiment

Early on, I told you my mission with this book: I want us to trade lonely and isolated lives that experience brief bursts of connectedness for intimately connected lives that experience only brief intervals of feeling alone.

If you have been stuck feeling lonely for a long time or if you have been a little lazy when it comes to your relationships or a little bit obstinate and rude toward your friends, it can be *really hard* to change those behaviors. **I hate to break it to you, but much of our problem isn't with other people. It's with us.** We must become the people we want in our lives. So how do people change?

Are you up for a little experiment? For the next five weeks, I want to help you connect with five people you're not deeply connected to at present.

———

As I mentioned in my book *Get Out of Your Head,* you and I tend to think the same negative, toxic thoughts day after day. In fact, 80 percent of our thoughts, researchers tell us, are negative. Studies also reveal that 95 percent of our thoughts are repetitive.[7] The same is true about our relationships and our behaviors. When we think the same thoughts, we manifest the same behaviors, and those behaviors impact our relationships in similar ways.

In the next section of this book, we're going to fight back against the isolated pattern of our lives by installing five practices that, coupled with God in the center of those interactions, will build healthier, deeper relationships.

When we moved to Dallas and started from scratch, I considered how I could re-create what I had seen around the world, how I could find my people and live in deeper, more regular, and life-giving community with them. I found five patterns that were consistent in villages and can be a part of our lives anywhere we live, from suburbs to Manhattan to apartments to small towns to college dorms.

Here is what we are going to build into our lives if you come with me on this journey:

- **Proximity.** Communal fires have been in the center of village life, bringing neighbors together to cook, to celebrate, to gather after dark and connect. Who do you see most often, and where?

- **Transparency.** Most of the world has never lived with locked doors and fences. And while that might be a necessity in our homes, it isn't a necessity in our relationships. Who can you most truly be yourself with?
- **Accountability to Others.** In many villages this looks like tribal elders, people who have permission to wallop you over the head when you are being an idiot! Village life causes you to live accountable to others. It isn't comfortable but it is transformative. Who are you living close to that has permission to wallop you when you need it?
- **A Shared Purpose.** Living together and working together creates bonds and is how most people

FIRE — Goal: Proximity / Barrier: Busyness

OPEN DOORS — Goal: Transparency / Barrier: Pain/Shame

ANVIL — Goal: Accountability / Barrier: Pride

SHOVEL — Goal: Shared Purpose / Barrier: Shallow/Small Talk

TABLE — Goal: Consistency / Barrier: Conflict

have lived in community. Who is near you already, working beside you, and how could you bring more purpose to the friendships you already have?

- **Consistency.** It takes time to build friendship and connection. We have to clock hours together over years. In Jesus's time, each school was made up of a small group of boys. We are the most transient generation of all time. How do we stay and commit and spend regular time with people, even if they hurt us?

In the chapters to come we will evaluate how these five simple practices could redefine the way we live in relationship to others. We'll look at the history of what made these simple practices within village life so instrumental in developing a sense of belonging and nurturing deeply committed, lifelong relationships. What brought them together? What kept those relationships tight all the way until the Industrial Revolution? And what can we graft into our lives to create a village existence of our own?

Let me be clear again: These practices are not the end goal. They are only tools to help you connect in deeper ways.

My big dream is that the patterns we'll be adopting will weave a culture of community into our daily lives, a way for us to put into practice this challenge from 1 John: "Let us love one another, for love is from God, and whoever loves has been born of God and knows God."[8]

That way of life is possible—with God.

So let's imagine together what that might look like.

What if we chose to do life in close proximity to each other?

What if we lived less guarded and more openhearted with each other?

What if we chose people in our lives who challenged us to be better each time we were together?

What if we shared a deeper purpose in our relationships?

What if we stayed instead of quitting each other when it gets difficult?

We are going to talk about it all. But I also am going to ask you to take a risk with me. At the end of each chapter in part 2, I'll give you an assignment. And if you take five weeks and engage with these five activities, I believe at the end of it you will have new friends.

You want to change your life? You want to stop living lonely? I'll hold your hand. **But you have to show up and put one foot in front of another here.** If you come with me, you will see change.

Let's do this.

PART

2

. . .

THE PATH TO
CONNECTION

. . .

I REACH OUT, BUT PEOPLE CAN'T COME OVER. THEY ARE TOO BUSY. I FINALLY STOPPED ASKING. —AMANDA

BUILDING RELATIONSHIPS TAKES A LOT OF TIME AND ENERGY THAT I DON'T HAVE MUCH LEFT OF. —JENN

I MOVED AWAY FROM MY PEOPLE FOR A BETTER JOB, AND I MISS THEM SO MUCH. —CAIT

WORKING FULL TIME AND BEING IN A NEW CITY AND AT A LARGE CHURCH, IT IS HARD TO CULTIVATE DEEP FRIENDSHIPS. —AMY

I TRY TO STAY IN TOUCH WITH MY FRIENDS, BUT HONESTLY, THEY'RE TOO CAUGHT UP IN THEIR OWN LIVES TO TAKE MUCH OF AN INTEREST IN MINE. —BRI

BETWEEN WORKING FORTY-PLUS HOURS, TAKING CARE OF A HOUSE, COMMUTING, FAMILY, HUSBAND, THERE IS JUST NOT MUCH TIME LEFT. IN THAT LITTLE TIME I DO CARVE OUT FOR A FRIEND, IT IS REALLY HARD TO TAKE THAT FRIENDSHIP PAST SUPERFICIAL CONVERSATION INTO DEEP CONVERSATIONS. —SARA R.

5.

CLOSE

■

🔥	FIRE	Goal: Proximity Barrier: Busyness

W HEN THE DOORBELL RANG AT 7:30 P.M., I HAD ALREADY
eaten dinner, changed into my long, comfy robe, and begun to
unwind from a stressful day. *Who could possibly be ringing our
doorbell right now?*

I opened the front door to find Lindsey, Kirk, and their
three kids, the whole lot looking like they'd just stepped out of
the pages of a magazine: perfectly coordinated, every hair on
every head in place, smiles as wide as Texas. "We just had our
family pictures taken," Lindsey explained. "I should have
texted you, but we were driving by, and I've been wanting Kirk
to see your patio furniture because we're wanting to get something similar, and, well, can we just take a peek and then let
you get back to your plans?"

I obviously didn't have "plans."

At the time, they were still newish friends, and I was very

aware I was in my robe. Glancing down at my attire, I had to laugh. "Come in!" I heard myself say.

The whole pack of us swept through the cluttered kitchen and living room and went outside to the patio. Zac and I insisted that they sit down and stay. They insisted that they didn't want to bother us, that, really, they should go.

Zac started a fire in the firepit, and we all sat down together, and they stayed.

They interrupted our nothing night, and their kids crawled all over us while we talked, and I never changed out of my robe. All of it was more heaven than my new-to-Dallas heart could contain.

About two hours into that fireside conversation, we realized we needed snacks. Lindsey and I went into the kitchen to grab whatever junk we could find and then returned to the fire, to our families, to the conversation at hand. I look back on that night now and realize that the unplanned nature of the whole thing took our relationship to a new level, a deeper level, a level that said, "Yeah, I know we don't yet know each other well, but I am going to be *that kind* of friend in your life."

The kind of friend who drops by unannounced.

The kind of friend kids can crawl all over without being told to stop.

The kind of friend who looks past your bathrobe and messy house.

The Magic of a Fire

Since the Stone Age, we humans have been building fires, and while there are plenty of practical reasons for this—we wanted cooked food, we needed to forge metal, we were hoping to stave off a bitterly cold winter, and more—one of the primary benefits of those fires has been the simple ambiance they afford. Firepit flames seem to mesmerize us, and we can kind of get lost in their trance.

Given that we spend most of our days strategizing, planning, working, and following through, there is a natural pull to sit down, to relax, to calm the mind, to chat. A fire gives us a place to do all these things. "Gathering around an evening fire is . . . an important opportunity for calm information exchange," wrote Christopher Lynn, associate professor of anthropology at the University of Alabama.

> During the day, biological rhythms produced by elevated cortisol and other stress hormones keep humans awake and provide the pre-coffee bump needed to be motivated and get things done. . . . But as cortisol levels drop in the evening, we're able to sit and relax. We're in a mood to tell and listen to stories.[1]

I remember reading of an anthropologist who spent nearly two hundred days living with the native people of Botswana and Namibia. She discovered that, while about three-fourths of the tribe's daytime conversations centered on work-related talk, more than three-fourths of their nighttime conversations—always held around a fire, incidentally—centered on spirituality or what the researcher called "enthralling stories." The tribespeople talked about adventures they'd had. And about elephants they'd encountered. And about politics, religion, and the dreams they had for their lives.[2]

———

Throughout history villages have gathered around fires to cook, to plan, to dance and sing, to be together after the kids are in bed. Yep. Fire has been the communal spot since the beginning of time. According to research published in *Proceedings of the National Academy of Sciences,* "ending the day around the campfire, where songs, stories and relationships blossomed, ultimately shaped cultures and perhaps even helped develop some of our ability to understand one another, cooperate and internalize culture."[3]

Fires bring us together. ***Real life, face to face, no phones, together.***

Five Friends. Five Miles.

———

It is not really an exaggeration to say that for the first months that we lived in Dallas, we were not invited anywhere. You know how when you've been living in the same place for a while, your biggest concern—assuming there's not a global pandemic—is knowing what to say yes to and what to say no to? Life feels so busy that at times you're sure that if your kids have one more thing they are required to attend, your whole universe might spin right off its axis.

So, take that reality and turn it, oh, 180 degrees, and you'll know what Dallas was like for us the first year we called it home. Zac and I rarely did anything. Our kids never did anything. Excitement was movie night at home.

One afternoon, on my way home from the grocery store, where I'd seen nobody I knew and had exactly zero conversations with another human being, I drove past a senior-living apartment situated half a mile from our house, and before I could stop them, tears sprang to my eyes.

I'll have no friends to live there with someday, because I have no friends.

Drama. I know.

I toyed for half a second with the idea of becoming a modern-day hermit, right there in the densely populated community of North Dallas. Who needed friends, anyway? Think of all the time I'd have, how much cleaner life would be. Things would be far simpler. No disappointments. No relational pain.

I could have done it, honestly . . . maybe . . . except for one detail I just couldn't shake: **we were not created to live alone.**

I thought about those Rwandan women who had a whole village worth of camaraderie, dozens and dozens of lifelong relationships at their disposal. And there in the seat of that rundown van, I thought, *If I could just have a fraction of that connectedness, I'd be happy. Five friends in five miles? I would totally settle for that.*

Five friends in five miles. This became my Dallas Friendship Plan. I set about looking for friends who lived within walking distance. I might not be able to rack up scores and scores of relational wins in Dallas, but surely I could at least find five friends who lived close by. I could make this work.

Five friends within five miles. Ready, set, go.

Your People Are Probably
Closer Than You Think

Now, before you put a For Sale sign in your yard, let's look for the friends who might be right under your nose.

The most common explanation I hear from people about why they don't have friends is they are too busy. But what if, instead of scheduling occasional lunch dates or starting some new monthly club, you looked around at what you already are doing and who you already are with?

My sister-in-law Ashley recently went on a four-day silent retreat, and while I suspected she was going to hate the experience, in an act of impressive self-restraint I held my tongue until she returned. "Well, what did you think?" I asked as we settled in on my back porch to analyze it all.

"It was . . . silent," Ashley said. "And also, pure torture."

"I knew it!" I beamed. "I *knew* that's how you'd feel."

We are both extroverts, and while I've been on plenty of silent retreats alone to write or to pray, trying to survive in silence with real live human beings around would be agonizing at best. I can do the "alone thing," no problem. It's just that when I'm supposed to behave as if I'm alone when there are perfectly lovely people around, I just can't relax.

We are *meant* to short-circuit when we are surrounded by people we aren't engaging with. It's *supposed* to make us feel tortured inside when we act alone in the context of perfectly good people we could be hanging out with and loving well. We should come away absolutely hating any experience that by design distances us from other human beings instead of helping us to draw near to each other. And yet far too many of us have adopted this as a lifestyle. We go through life barely noticing the people God has put right in our paths, insisting that we're all alone in the world, that nobody cares, and that we're doing just fine on our own. The truth is this: we are meant to be emotionally close to the people we are physically close to.

Be close to those we're close to—that's my goal for us. And it's admittedly a stretch goal. Because most of us choose to hold on to friends from past residences and past lives, believing that since nobody who is right here in front of us will ever measure up to those precious people, why bother making new friends?

Or we say we are too busy to build new relationships, when we are actually around people that could be more than acquaintances if we invited them into our lives.

Or we center every moment of every day on our nuclear family members so that we never even allow ourselves to dream about having caring, intimate, non-family friends.

Or we believe we need to have absolutely everything in common with people and be in the same life stage before we even consider they could become close friends.

Or we move constantly, we never settle down, and we are always looking for the next adventure, next roommate, next church, next job. We don't truly commit to a place and a handful of people. **If you are trying to make friendship an addendum to your busy schedule, it will never work.**

You have to build it as you're going. Relationships should arise out of your everyday places and your everyday activities.

Proximity is a starting place for intimacy.

Yes, I have deep sister-friends spread all over the country, but those relationships will always take more effort. It's hard to "run a casserole over" when the world falls apart for one of them. Many of my long-distance friends are forever friends to me, and I have a handful that I will never let go as long as I live. **But we all need a network of regular people who are present in our daily lives.**

Hebrews commands us to consistently make time together: "And let us consider how to stir up one another to love and good works, not neglecting to meet together, as is the habit of some, but encouraging one another, and all the more as you see the Day drawing near."[4] The writer is speaking here of the church, which we will discuss in greater detail later, but when this exhortation was written, "church" was defined as a group of people, not a building for a once-a-week gathering. The Church was a local group of interdependent people who loved God and each other. They did everything together. They ate together, prayed together, encouraged each other, and sold goods so that they could take care of each other.[5]

To build a lifestyle in which we are consistently present for one another like this, we need to do three key things.

STEP 1: *Notice Who Is Already*
Right in Front of You

Consider the people who you see regularly at your school or your church or your job or your neighborhood or a kid's sports team or a book club. Could it be that there are close friendships waiting for you there?

Right now, get a blank piece of paper and draw scattered circles for each of the activities and venues you frequent over the course of a given week. Label each circle with the location or activity. Next to each circle, write the names of people you interact with in each place. Now think about each of those people in terms of potential friendships.

Who do you enjoy being around?

Who do you share some things in common with?

Who seems genuinely interested in you?

Go back over your list of acquaintances and highlight ten names of people you could see yourself investing in on a deeper level. Pray over those ten highlighted names, and ask God to help you decide on the three to five people to pursue deep relationships with. Who are those people? Circle each name with a red pen.

Your map might look something like the example on the facing page.

The truth of my relational situation when I moved to Dallas was that I knew some friends. The problem was that, while those people all lived in Dallas, few of them lived within a

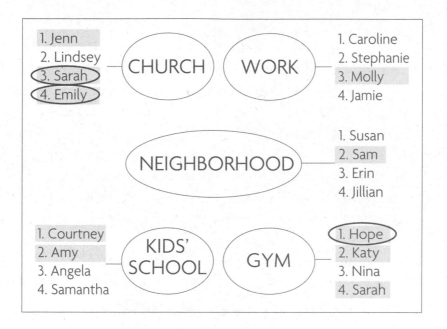

1. Jenn
2. Lindsey
3. Sarah
4. Emily

CHURCH

WORK

1. Caroline
2. Stephanie
3. Molly
4. Jamie

NEIGHBORHOOD

1. Susan
2. Sam
3. Erin
4. Jillian

1. Courtney
2. Amy
3. Angela
4. Samantha

KIDS' SCHOOL

GYM

1. Hope
2. Katy
3. Nina
4. Sarah

half-hour drive of our new home. As is the case with Austin (and hundreds of other metropolises throughout our country), Dallas is an urban sprawl made up of countless bedroom communities, subdivisions, neighborhoods, and parts of town, each connected to the next by tangled spaghetti mounds of interstates and freeways. To drive from one side of the city to the other takes planning, strategy, and time. Had I settled for simply reconnecting with all the people I already knew, I would have been replicating the terrible reality I'd fallen into in Austin: namely, living so far away from my people that they never felt like my people at all. If a friend—or I—was having a meltdown on an average Tuesday night, we needed to be able to get to each other—fast.

———

I realized I had to quit viewing everyone in my new neighborhood and at my kids' schools, church, and Conner's football games as nameless strangers. **I needed to start viewing them as friends in the making.**

So, that's step 1 for both you and me: Start seeing the people right in front of us as friends—or *potential* friends, at least.

This next part is where things get a little awkward.

STEP 2: Put Yourself Out There

It's rare that someone will take the initiative in friendship, so quit waiting for that to happen. Everybody is busy, and few people are prioritizing deep connection. In other words, plan to go first.

Connection takes stepping out and being intentional again and again. If you're thinking, *I've done that for so long, and nobody is reciprocating,* let me gently encourage you to be sad for exactly one minute and then to get over it and own that role. **You will never have friends unless you are willing to consistently initiate.** Be the one who reaches out. Initiate and initiate again. You can't expect to have friends unless you get good at this. Even though it's frustrating. Even though it's awkward.

It will almost always be awkward.

It was awkward when I reached out to that camp counselor after two and a half decades, not to thank her for being a positive influence during my teen years, but to ask her to be friends. I imagined her sitting there at the coffee shop across from me thinking, *How desperate must this poor woman be, to have to dig all the way down to her teenage relationships to find a friend?* I didn't care. I was desperate.

It was awkward when I spilled my neediness to poor Caroline Parker, the college student who thought she was coming to my house to be interviewed for a babysitter position, not to be my therapist.

It was awkward when we showed up at our new small group and shared the real story of our lives with complete strangers.

But each time over the past three years that I have chosen to drop the facade of "I'm great, thanks," and initiate conversations about how I'm really doing and what the other person really needs, God has handed me the most life-giving exchanges imaginable. In the wake of initiating, inviting the person to coffee, being willing to spill my guts, and asking the hard questions, real friendships began to form.

We go first. We keep initiating.

We see enough of Jesus's life in the Gospels to know that He was an incredible initiator. He noticed people. He stopped for a conversation. He even invited Himself over to Zacchaeus's house for dinner.

I have been blessed to be able to do some work in Israel, and the thing that surprised me most is the tight radius within which most of Jesus's ministry took place. Israel is a small country, roughly the size of New Jersey. Only five miles separate Bethlehem from Jerusalem. Communities were located intentionally so that people could return easily to the temple. We could sit on a boat in the Sea of Galilee and see the various places where Jesus spent most of His life. Most of the disciples lived just a few miles from each other, and most of their travels were day trips on foot.

Jesus lived small and simply, doing life with those immediately around him, but those few people's lives would affect the whole world. He prioritized proximity, His family, intimate meals, and fireside chats. That wasn't revolutionary in biblical times. It's just how people lived.

And it mattered. People in small towns, living life together, was essential to the way the Church would grow and spread. The entire Church was birthed from a few uneducated fishermen and their friends, and it reached to the ends of the earth. And yes, someone had to take the gospel to the world. Paul and the apostles would travel and spread the good news, but all along the way, they settled into community contexts, staying with families, being invested in and supported by local churches.

Community should, in its truest form, reflect aspects of who God is and how He loves. Which brings me to a question: Who has God put in your life—here and now and right under your nose—that you haven't really connected with yet?

Remember, the enemy wants to shut you down, make you afraid to initiate, cause you to not prioritize the people right in front of you. He wants us to live surrounded by people but never deeply connected to them, so we don't change, we don't grow, we don't even fully live—and we mostly end up stuck in self-pity about how we don't have any friends when dozens of people in front of us certainly would welcome someone reaching out to them at the very least.

In case you need help seeing the people in your life from this perspective, the following list will get you started. Granted, it isn't exhaustive. But hopefully it will put words to what you need in the little team you are gathering around you—and help you notice the people who may already be filling key roles. These individuals may be of varying ages and cross your path in various ways, but the point is to look for people with certain qualities to play different roles in your life, not just seek out two to three people who are exactly like you and expect them to meet all your relational needs.

A village of people meeting different needs and loving you in different ways provides a fuller, richer way to live. And these people probably exist somewhere around you already, maybe family members or neighbors or people at your church or your work? You just have to spot what gifts they bring to your life and also own the role you play for others. What do you bring to your friendships?

Here are a few types of people to look for in your life.

THE SAGE

This is the friend who listens, prays, and advises. They love for you to bring them a problem. They carry godly wisdom earned through study and/or life experience. They are safe and trustworthy. The apostle Paul was a sage friend to Timothy.

THE ENCOURAGER

This is the cheerleader, the friend who believes in you. They see the good in you and call it out. It is easy for them to speak hope when you are discouraged. They see the best in life and people. This person oozes belief and support.

THE FOXHOLE FRIEND

This is just a good companion. This friend gets their hands dirty with you. If you have an idea, they are all in! They will fight for you and fight beside you. I have a friend, Jenn Jett Barrett, who calls herself a dream defender and has helped along almost every dream I have ever built. Your foxhole friend may not use words to express what you mean to her, but she'll be right beside you and share in whatever trouble you get into.

THE CHALLENGER

This is the friend who isn't afraid to tell you the truth. They won't let you settle, and they will kick you in the booty if you get off track. They might not be your easiest friend, and you might have to work through conflict here and there, but they make you better every time.

THE FUN ONE

This is the friend that brings the party. They might not have a two-hour debate with you about a theological issue, but they will make sure you laugh often. They are spontaneous and pull people together and say something inappropriate that interrupts whatever bad mood you find yourself stuck in.

THE PLANNER

This is the organized and thoughtful friend who makes sure you get together and makes sure the bill gets split up correctly during girls' night out. She starts the meal train email and remembers your birthday.

My mom is a fantastic planner friend. She hosts the showers and drops by with a meal when you get sick. Last month, another friend and I were on Mom's back porch catching up, and in a matter of two hours she had brought us something to drink, then a full charcuterie board, followed by blankets because it was getting chilly. When I was young, and her attention to detail was directed toward my life, I was bugged! But now, being around my mom feels like visiting a classy hotel. We both felt her love, and I love it!

My mom sometimes gushes about how proud she is of me, but the main way my mom shows her love is by inviting my friends and me into her back-porch life.

I'M CERTAINLY NOT SUGGESTING that you rush out and start interviewing acquaintances to play these specific roles. What I'm saying is that within your sphere of influence someone is likely already playing one or more of these roles, even if you haven't yet thought of them as a friend. **No one can be your everything, but everyone has something to say,** something to teach you, and something to bring to your life.

Look for it.

Do you have someone in your life who is habitually encouraging? Thank that person.

What about someone who is incredibly wise? Ask for more input from her.

Do you know someone who is impossibly fierce, who seems unafraid of life? Sort out a way to dive into some purposeful project together. Make a memory doing something that counts.

Thank your planner friend for initiating gatherings that are meaningful and sweet.

Bless that friend who always, always picks up your call.

Express appreciation to the one who still sends you birthday cards in the mail.

Tell that challenging friend that you're grateful for a divergent point of view.

Even if it means disrupting the current easy rhythm of a casual relationship, go ahead and take the initiative to start going deeper with these people who already are present in your life. You may as well get comfortable with awkward, because we're about to take it a step further.

STEP 3: *Start Great Conversations*

If you aren't sure how to get past shallow conversations, please know that you're not alone.

Sometimes I will leave a girls' night thinking that I had a great time, but for some reason I'll get home and have this kind of sick feeling that I can't quite place. More often than not, the feeling stems from what our conversations were about.

Often those conversations are too shallow. Talking about a work project or your kids is fine, but I won't leave feeling known or truly knowing you. **To have deeper conversations, we have to learn the art of asking more intentional questions.** I will give you more on this in the next chapter, but here are two to try out:

"What are you longing for?"

"What is making you anxious?"

And when someone shares with you what they are longing for and what is making them anxious, sit with those feelings; don't try and fix anything. Practice words like "I'm sorry" or "What do you need from me right now?"

Questions like that bring fresh depth to your conversation. Maybe kids or work still come up, but you will be getting closer to how that makes the person feel rather than settling for a news report from her life.

I honestly think that most people just don't know how to ask good questions and how to genuinely share their hearts. That's why conversations often drift toward complaining and gossip. We all know how to do those things!

You'll recall that during those first few hours in Dallas I

was sitting on the floor of my empty new house having an outright panic attack. Now, let's contrast that scene with another, more recent one involving several people who have stumbled their way into my life since that hollow-house moment four years ago: Ashley, my sister-in-law turned safest friend, who now lives two blocks away; my dear friend Lindsey, whom I met through Ashley and then realized I'd gone to Sunday school with during our elementary school years in Little Rock, Arkansas; Callie, who I met through a girl I discipled in college; and Jennie E., a new friend I met because our sons are friends at school.

The group of us had been doing a Bible study on prayer together. One week Ashley suggested it would be cool for us to sit in my backyard around my firepit and *actually* pray. Novel idea, right?

I invited my friend Davy to join us. I'd first met Davy through her stunning music, before we lived close enough to hang out. I'd heard some of her songs and knew that she led worship for a church in Mississippi, so I asked if she would come along on one of the tours I did for IF:Gathering.

"I'd love to come!" Four simple words—that's all it took for us to become more like sisters than friends. And before we got off the phone, she told me, "I might be living in Dallas by then."

"I live in Dallas!" I said, having no idea she was coming to take a job at our church. And now here she was, close enough to be part of our community of friends. When I invited Davy to our fireside prayer gathering, she said, "Ooh! Can I bring my keyboard?"

So the six of us sat by that fire, and we prayed, we confessed sin, we sang, we cried, we laughed. As I scanned the faces belonging to the people sitting around that fire with me, I was left undone by that unexpected, relationally rich night.

I wanted to stand on my chair and shout, "Look, world! I have friends!"

It feels so ridiculous to even type those words, but that's exactly how I felt.

With a crackling fire, Davy's singing in our ears, prayerful, hopeful words being spoken, and a blanket of stars overhead, I rested into the connection I'd been craving, that feeling that I'm not all alone in this world. Four years of building and investing and choosing connection over isolation, and I had my people.

CREATE A GATHERING PLACE

—

HOW DO WE GET BACK TO LIVING IN AUTHENTIC, CONNECTED community the way generations of people have lived and the way Jesus calls us to live?

Researchers say that to grow an acquaintance to a good friend takes clocking two hundred hours together.[6] So here's the first challenge of our big experiment to build meaningful community: **build an environment to have great conversations.**

During the COVID-19 quarantine of 2020, Zac and I often

took walks around the neighborhood, and one of my favorite sights was a front yard stuffed with six cheap, plastic, turquoise Adirondack chairs, all placed in a ring. On one of the chairs was always perched a bottle of mosquito spray, as if to say, "Pandemic, quarantine, not even stinkin' mosquitoes are gonna keep us from getting together!"

That's why I want you to start by getting a firepit. A basic one is not as expensive as you might think. If a fire is not possible where you live, then build your gathering spot, your place where people can congregate. Get a patio or picnic table or stick a couple of comfy outdoor chairs somewhere facing each other. However it works best for your particular home, create your gathering spot and stock it with whatever you need. We personally keep on hand dozens of supplies for s'mores at all times.

And then you invite. You spontaneously but also deliberately and regularly start inviting people in your everyday world. People will say no, and you keep inviting anyway.

And then you ask real questions, the kind that make everyone just uncomfortable enough that you might actually get to know them. You go first and volunteer your answers to get things rolling. Then all of you sit together and you laugh and you clock some of those two hundred hours you need to grow those relationships into what's considered real friends.

Remember, you aren't the only one craving community. Everyone is craving it. So be the one who makes it happen!

Ideas for Building Relationships with Proximity

· · · · · ·

- Buy a firepit and invite over friends who live close to your house.
- Invite a friend to run errands with you.
- Invite someone at work to walk to the vending machine with you.
- Who do you see when you are walking your dog? Talk to them and walk together. Note their name (and their dog's name!) down in your phone so you don't forget it.
- Introduce yourself to strangers in the coffee shop.
- Go up to the people sitting by themselves at church and invite them to lunch.
- If you are new to a city, ask the person next to you at church something like, "Where is the best place to get Thai in Dallas?" And then invite them to join you there for a meal.
- Take the newest person in your office out to lunch.
- Ask another family to join yours for celebratory ice cream after your kid's sporting event.
- Frequent a restaurant and learn your waiter's name and ask how you can pray for him.

- Look for everyday things to do with people. Ask your friend if you can help her fold laundry.
- If you're a young mom, go grocery shopping with another young mom. Yes, with all your kids in tow.

BUT WHAT ABOUT . . .

. . . my long-distance friends? Are you saying I can't be friends with them?

No! Some of my dearest friends live nowhere near me. But the fact remains that I need somebody to bring me a casserole when I am floundering in crisis or stress, and I need someone who can look me in the eyeballs and call me out on what I'm not saying. I need someone who pops in spontaneously, makes me get dressed, and pulls me out to have some fun when I get depressed. And my people need me to do the same for them. So, while I will never lose my longtime, long-distance friends, I can't function well without friends who live close by. Neither can you.

. . . the reality that I move a lot for work?

The power of a plan and patterns for living is that they set you up to live well, wherever you are. As someone who just started over, I can tell you that this plan has worked for me. So even if you have to execute this plan at lightning speed because you

won't be in your current location long, do it. No point in living
lonely, even for a year.

*. . . when I try to go deeper in conversation
and the vulnerability is not reciprocated?*

I get it. Some people don't have this capacity. Move on, keep
trying. Don't quit. Don't get discouraged. Don't make it a bigger deal than it is. Don't give in to fear. Just go to the next
person. If that doesn't work out, go to the next person.

Remember to look for your people in unexpected places.
Life stage doesn't matter. Age doesn't matter. Find the people
who are following after Jesus, and then go with them.

I HAVE A HARD TIME
TRUSTING. —PATTI

I'M AFRAID I MIGHT
NEED MORE THAN
I CAN GIVE. —KIM

I'M UNABLE TO LET GO
OF OLD FRIENDSHIPS
THAT HURT ME. —CHRISTY

I'VE BEEN REJECTED SO
MUCH IN THE PAST.
—BROOKE

I FEEL LIKE A BURDEN,
SO I JUST DON'T GO DEEP.
—MOLLY

I FEEL LIKE I HAVE TO
PRETEND THAT I AM OKAY
OR BE JUDGED. —STEFANIE

6.

SAFE

■

OPEN DOORS   Goal: Transparency
Barrier: Pain/Shame

*I*HAVE LOST FRIENDS BECAUSE I HAVEN'T DONE WHAT I AM about to tell you to do. I wrote this chapter through many tears, knowing that I am terrible at what I am going to ask you to do here.

I've been racking my brain, trying to remember how the conversation came about or why we were talking about such a deep and meaningful thing in the first place. As best I can recall, my friend Jessica and I were wrapping up an interview for my podcast by talking about how much we missed each other after my move to Dallas. I think she said something about being worried about losing our friendship across the miles. "You'll never lose me!" I said to her, meaning it. She was one of my most beloved friends when we both lived in Austin, and with barely three hours' drive time separating us, I figured we would keep a good thing going for years.

We were both kind of laughing—in that sentimental way that women do when they're saying something important but don't want to start crying—when I posed this question: "Jess, tell me how I can be a better friend to you?"

I thought she'd reply with something along the lines of, "Oh, I don't know, Jennie, how about we set up a weekly phone chat?" Or, "Let's get a girls' weekend on the calendar." Or, "Text me more often than you think you should." I thought she would answer my question with a task list of sorts, a few things I could do for her.

She didn't answer that way at all.

"You never need anything," Jessica said. "You never need me. You never need anything from me. *I want you to need me more.*"

All the oxygen emptied from my tiny recording closet. Tears filled my eyes as my hands fell to my lap. My mouth was hovering over the microphone, but no words were coming out. What was I supposed to say to that? What could I possibly say? What one of my dearest friends needed from me wasn't more attention, more camaraderie, more support. **What she needed from me was more of me.**

The one problem? I wasn't sure I could say yes to that.

As badly as the end of that conversation went, the worst was yet to come. Stopped at a traffic light on my way home from the office that afternoon, a haunting feeling came over me. I'd been sickened by Jessica's response because it told me that the entire time we'd been friends, she'd felt like the road between us was something of a one-way street. But more agonizing than this first realization was the second realization that hit: *I've had this same conversation before.* Jessica's words were painfully familiar. I'd lost other friendships for this same reason.

Eighteen months earlier my friendship with Courtney had blown up. And the reason she'd cited then was the same one Jessica articulated now: "I hate that, to know what's really going on with you, I have to read your Instagram. *You never need me.*"

She went on to say that she needed a break from me. "I don't think I can be in a relationship like this," she explained, "where I'm the only one who is being authentic, where I'm the only one who ever has needs."

I remember being confused. *Am I really such an impossible person to be friends with? Is this her deal? My deal? Are we equally to blame?* For days—weeks, maybe—I reeled. I felt embarrassed. I truly thought of Courtney as one of my closest friends. And also, I felt ashamed. How had I become so closed off to people I cared about? **Where had the transparent part of me gone—and when?**

It's Easier to Put Up Walls

Here is who I appear to be: gregarious, extroverted, chatty, inclusive, outgoing, generous with time and heart, loving, caring, a connector, great at parties, comfortable with people, content in my relational world.

Here is who I really am: all those things, until it goes deep. Then I hedge. Or distract. Or bail.

Don't get me wrong. I love to go deep about you. I'm just

not that interested in divulging the truest parts of me. It feels selfish somehow. Greedy. Needy. Wrong. It feels like I'm wasting your time. Or sucking up too much oxygen. Or saying more than is prudent. Or talking when I should be listening. I guess maybe, too, I hate not being understood. What if I share the deepest parts of me and you look at me confused? Or worse, you try to fix me or change me?

These are all my reasons for asking you the probing questions and listening with sparkling eyes, shoulders hunched toward you in interest, mind hanging on your every word. But the fact is, I'm guarded. The truth is, I've been hurt.

Back when we were just kids, Zac heard about me from a friend of his, who said, "Zac, you'll love her. She wears her heart on her sleeve."

The friend meant it as high praise. If I felt something, I said it. I owned it. I was an open book. Zac wouldn't have to guess how I was doing; I was openhearted and honest. That really is who I was back then: forthright, defenseless, unafraid. But that kind of living kept burning me. As a young mom, being honest with a few friends about how hard parenting and our marriage had become resulted in judgment instead of understanding. Because I was a pastor's wife, the struggles I disclosed to a friend in private became fodder for church gossip and were used against both Zac and me in uncomfortably public ways. I once shared about a success with a friend, aching for someone to celebrate with me. Instead, my motives were immediately questioned. I recall dozens of other occasions when, despite my good intentions, things I said came back to haunt me.

Over time, after relational hurts stacked themselves high

enough, something in me hesitated when someone really wanted to know me. Inadvertently I started a building project. Without much thought, I erected tall walls with locked doors around my life. I'd reveal enough so people felt close to me but not give anyone enough to use against me. I'd cut out little windows here and there, so people felt like they knew me, but I lost my openheartedness and began to live in a protective way.

WE HIDE Because of Pain

It would be easy to keep reading about my friendship dysfunctions and not apply anything to your life. But since we agreed to take this journey together, I'd like to give you a more active role. And so, I will ask you: What are your past relational pains? In what ways have you been hurt?

- Have you opened up to a friend, only to have that friend use what you shared against you?
- Have you drawn close to a group of friends and eventually found yourself on the outside of that group?
- Have you felt judged because you didn't measure up to some standard, spoken or unspoken?
- Have you shared a struggle only to receive a sideways glance of judgment, made to feel like you are the only one who really struggles?
- Have you invited and invited and shared and shared and invested and invested, and then when you need something, no one is there?

"After being burned, backstabbed, lied to, and otherwise betrayed," one of my Instagram followers told me, "I have a hard time trusting anyone . . . letting them come inside my walls."

Yep. I get the *walls* thing. It's safer behind those walls.

Walls are a luxury, a privilege. I learned this in Haiti while standing on the hill that overlooks a tent city, located a short two-hour flight from the coast of an affluent part of Florida. Blue tarps flapping in the wind concealed thousands of souls who, years after the big earthquake, still were displaced. They don't have walls in that community.

I've noticed a similar reality in Africa, where I've visited dozens of huts. Guess how many huts have permanent walls, let alone doors with locks? None I have seen. Beyond the lack of physical privacy, vulnerability and transparency are an intentional part of village life. People who are simply trying to survive the rigors of daily life don't have the capacity to both hold pain and shut others out. They don't have the luxury of a closed, locked door . . . of tall, thick walls . . . of staying alone. **They need each other, and they know it.**

But here is what I want to tell you: While it's true that those people living in tough spots all over the world don't choose vulnerability as much as vulnerability chooses them, it's also true that vulnerability is choosing you and me. It's asking us to come out of hiding and engage. To quit living behind our walls.

While admittedly painful—excruciating even, depending on the day—the lesson I'm learning right now is that **vulnerability is the soil for intimacy, and what waters intimacy is tears.** Real, raw, gut-wrenching honesty about the fight that made you want to leave your spouse last night, or the addiction to pornography or sex that is eating you alive, or the abortion you have never shared, or the small stuff that makes you cry, the anxiety you feel when you think of your kids going to college, or the ache you feel to be married.

I wish I could tell you it worked the other way. I wish I could tell you that a friendship built solely on laughter and fun and lighthearted gatherings and good times would stand the test of time, would nourish the needs of your soul. I am good at all that stuff, you know?

But bare-my-soul intimacy? Not so much.

And yet whenever I hide behind my walls with the doors locked tight to keep out the potential of being misunderstood, or wronged, or devastated, or disappointed, or disillusioned, or mistreated, or hurt, I'm also keeping out the good things—everything we are built to crave: being encouraged, being held accountable, being seen, being loved, being known.

We all crave friends in the trenches who call us midcry and whom we call midcry, friends who don't quit and don't judge, friends who make us feel understood, seen, and challenged and remind us of our God and our hope, friends who compel us to get out of our robes and into our lives and callings—and none of that is possible until we risk letting our walls fall.

We must risk pain to have this kind of deep connection in our lives.

WE HIDE Because of Shame

The enemy loves us to self-protect, and sometimes he will use our pain and sometimes he will use our shame. If you read my previous book *Get Out of Your Head,* you'll remember that, alone in the dark, the enemy can tell us all kinds of lies about ourselves, our God, our reality. He lures us behind walls with a sneaky word that sounds true and worms its way into our thoughts to become a belief about ourselves.

Shame.

If you're like me, you just winced when you read that word. You don't risk transparency now because you've shared your struggles before and "friends" punished you for being so real.

One of the enemy's favorite lies is the lie of shame, because the cost of shame is connection. I said earlier that, in the beginning, Adam and Eve had everything they needed from God. They were loved by God and were perfectly safe with each other. And still, they went off the rails. They chose their own way and broke their relationship with God and one another.

Satan. A choice. An apple. Shame. Immediate shame.

And how did they react? Genesis says they hid. They covered their shame and nakedness with leaves. They didn't want God to find them.

But, of course, God found them.

God wanted them to come out of sin and hiding and shame and come back into relationship with Him. But God is just and righteous, and He could not tolerate sin with no consequence. Sin required payment, and the price was death. That day He set in motion an answer to it all. He covered the nakedness and shame of Adam and Eve with clothes made from animal skin. It was a picture of the gospel, a promise that one day the blood sacrifice of a Lamb would cover our sins once and for all.

This remains God's desire, that we would be in right relationship with Him. This is the story of God. He loves us so much that even when we turn away, He fights to get us back, to make us right with Him. He values us so much, and He has set us in our places and created us for connection and purposes that are beyond what we can imagine. He does all that because He is good. He is so loving and powerful, and He wants to share Himself with us.

Since all this is true, we need never again be in bondage to shame. We have been made beautifully and totally free.

But we forget that this is so. We listen to the devil's lying whispers that lead to shame. Add to that shame the pain caused by others, and even if in our hearts we believe God's truth, we decide it's safer to build the walls. Sigh.

This is why when a friend texts a last-minute invitation to hang out, you decline, crawl into your bed, and turn on Netflix again. It's why even when a safe friend asks how you're doing, you spit back a reflexive (and generally untrue), "Great! How are you?" It's why I built walls without realizing it and continually made sure to be there for friends but never let them be there for me.

Shame is also why it feels like you get hit with arrows when you dare to peek out of your carefully built protective structure. Because shame can make people mean. While some of us hide behind walls of kindness and hospitality, others seek protection through hardness and cruelty, preemptively striking to avoid being hurt yet again.

We think the root problem of our isolation is chronic

busyness or tech addiction or broken families or the Church, **but the problem is inside all of us.** It was, and it is, and it will continue to be, until Jesus returns.

Is your marriage difficult?

Are you stuck in pornography or an obsession with your appearance?

Have you held on to hate and unforgiveness toward someone?

Are you trapped in debt that no one knows about?

Are you chronically angry toward your kids?

Do you doubt the faith you grew up holding?

The enemy's strategy is to push us deep into shame and sin and to make us feel so isolated and guilty that we would never admit our struggle aloud. Research tells us that we begin feeling shame between fifteen and eighteen months of age.[1] Meaning, we experience shame before we even have words for it. Over time this tendency erodes our trust in God and fractures our relationships with people.

The devil is good at his job. Not only does he use shame to strip us of connection and community, but his whisper invades our thinking and multiplies the pain: *It's your own fault that you're alone.*

Ugh. It isn't enough to feel alone. We feel guilty that it's our fault!

Pain and shame compel us to hide behind walls of self-protection.

Eventually, we grow lonely behind those walls and venture out.

_____

But other hurt, sinful people are wandering out of their walls and—*Bam!*—we get hurt again.

So we go back to hiding and the cycle spins on.

How do we break free?

To Be Fully Loved Requires Being Fully Known

Only when we let down our guards and allow ourselves to be known can we get over ourselves and get on with loving people. Love changes us and changes others. Love takes strangers and makes families. Love heals wounds and empty spaces in us that we never dreamed could be filled. God is love, and when we choose to cooperate with Him, we get to carry His love to people who are deeply desperate for it.

But it all starts with being known. I can tell any stranger on the street that I love her, and it will mean absolutely nothing. Why? Because I don't know her. My words are an empty platitude. But when I say to my son, who just confessed something he did wrong, "I love you!" well, that means everything.

We have no use for empty platitudes. It's the "I know you *and* I love you" that we crave.

It's why I love the gospel. It's the story where God rescues us from hiding. He restores us and tells us that "there is therefore now no condemnation for those who are in Christ Jesus."[2] And because we are restored and have full access to our God, a God who forgives, we have the tools to change the cycle of hiding.

Jesus said that she who has been forgiven much, loves much.[3] So, too, the things that sent us into hiding are the very tools God redeems to pull us out of hiding and so that, in love, we can go pull other people out of hiding.

Hurting people hurt others.

But equally true is that only forgiven people can truly forgive.

It's a whole new way to live.

We have to become friends who call each other out of hiding. "If we walk in the light, as he is in the light, we have fellowship with one another, and the blood of Jesus, his Son, purifies us from all sin."[4] We come into the light. We risk transparency. And we create a safe space for others to do the same.

How to Make Transparency a Way of Life

When you have been in the dark for a long time, stepping into the light can leave you blinking and confused. So I imagine you have a few questions, such as:

Do I really share everything? Yes. With the right safe, few, vetted people. You really do share everything. But not with everyone. Look back at the circles from chapter 4 and remember that we are working toward an inner circle of three to five people who know it all. **Your whole village doesn't need to know everything.** Only those committed to walking with you through your everyday life and deepest struggles qualify here.

What if the other person doesn't reciprocate with candor of her own? Try to find out why your friend doesn't feel safe being transparent. Ask great questions and keep trying, if this is one of your safe people. A lot of people (like me! 🙂) aren't great at this. They honestly need practice. Don't give up.

Do I need to give people permission to do this with me? Yes! You have to have the awkward conversation of saying, "I want you to be one of my people!"

How do you move past all the shallow conversations? I'll show you. We talked a little about great conversations in the last chapter, but let's get even more specific with a little Conversation 101 training.

Right up front let me say you should expect this to be awkward. Given how superficial our culture has become, there is no way to deepen a friendship without a bit of clumsy give and take. Instead of fearing it or denying it or explaining it away, how about we just own it? If you sense that a person is safe, then try these six steps for having a deep conversation. And remember, don't take yourself too seriously!

1. **Plan a get-together** for when you will be (mostly) uninterrupted and distraction-free.
2. **Prepare your friend** that you'd like to have an intentionally deeper conversation than you two normally enjoy. Say, "I really want to share some

things going on in my life right now." Or, if it's a small group of people, then say, "Hey, can we talk about what's really going on in our lives tonight?"

3. **Lead the conversation.** Express why you want to go deeper. Share a difficulty in your life. Be as vulnerable as you can because others will only go as deep and vulnerable as you go. When you share honestly, it will often give your people the desire to be honest in return. After you go first, ask the other person or people what feels hard in life right now.

4. **Resist the temptation to solve.** In a conversational manner, consistently repeat to your friend what you hear her saying. But do not interrupt. Wait until there is a clear pause before you feed back what you're hearing, offer your perspective, or ask another question. To build deep friendships will require a lot of intentional, active listening. If you have a perspective to offer, ask for permission to share it.

5. **Affirm your friend** following your conversation, and express how much the back-and-forth meant to you.

6. **Plan a follow-up gathering.**

One other piece of advice for practicing transparency: tell people exactly what you need from them. Most people are not accustomed to these conversations, but don't let their first reaction cause you to withdraw. If you want them to listen, then ask them to listen. If you want them to help you solve the problem, then ask them to help you solve the problem. **Tell people how to show up for you. And let them express how you can show up for them.**

Throwing Open the Doors

After that conversation with my friend Jessica, who told me during the podcast interview that to be a better friend I needed to need her more, I realized I'd had enough. I was sick of being careful. Censored. Safe. I knew that I wanted to change. I was a relational toddler in this area who wanted to grow and mature. The question was *how*.

What worked for toddlers was going to have to work for me: stumble and fall and stumble and fall and get back up again. This was year one in Dallas, and the two people I spent the most time with were my sister-in-law Ashley and my call-me-midcry, stop-by-rather-than-text friend Lindsey. They unknowingly became my relationship trainers. I studied the kinds of questions they asked, the kinds of liberties they took, the way they shared everything they were going through and processing without so much as batting an eye.

I realize how awkward it all sounds. Maybe I should have titled this book *How to Win Friends by Being Awkward*. But I am letting you into my internal crazy because I don't think I'm the only person who has recognized herself as stunted relationally to some extent. Granted, you and I may be stunted in different ways. Maybe your battle is that you are too needy, exhaustingly so, and don't know how to give. Or maybe you are too careless with the stories of others, using someone else's struggle to try to make yourself look better. Or maybe you wall off because you don't want to deal with the pressure of having others need you.

Or maybe your friend group that used to be a safe place for transparency has become just a space to grumble and complain with no healthy goal or end. In the next chapter we'll talk about this in a deeper way, but let me say now that thoughtless transparency isn't the goal, lest we make an idol out of our struggle and sin. No, we live known so that we can change and grow together. There is a purpose to the candor, and that purpose is for our good.

So, really, what's right to share?

Before a lunch with some new friends I sat down with my journal and my phone; I reviewed the previous week's obligations, activities, and events; and I scribbled down on a sticky note a few things I could vulnerably open up about. (I know. I am such a dork. But I was trying!) These were intimate things, honest things I'd be prepared to share.

We got to the restaurant and ordered, and then came that fifteen-minute lull when normal, relationally high-functioning people speak candidly about what's going on in their lives—not their Instagram lives, but their real lives. This is where I generally stick to asking questions—sparkly eyes, shoulders curled forward, attentive, the whole bit—but today, I was committed to engaging in a different way.

Now, I admit that as I divulged what I'd prepared to share, the handful of things that weren't exactly going well that week, I felt incredibly self-conscious, constantly wondering if I was sharing the right kinds of things, if I was dominating the conversation, and if I was making a fool of myself. But I plowed ahead, remembering that if I didn't take steps forward, I would stay right where I was. And right where I was wasn't a place I wanted to live.

But here's the thing:

you will only be as close to a friend as you are vulnerable with her.

And not to be a downer, but vulnerable people get hurt. Here is where you may be thinking, *I am better off going my own way and doing my own thing. At least my heart will stay intact.*

Or, *I will be civil. I will even be cordial. But authentically connected? Nope. Been there. Done that. And it's not for me.*

"To love at all is to be vulnerable," C. S. Lewis famously wrote.

> Love anything and your heart will be wrung and possibly broken. If you want to make sure of keeping it intact you must give it to no one, not even an animal. Wrap it carefully round with hobbies and little luxuries; avoid all entanglements. Lock it up safe in the casket or coffin of your selfishness. But in that casket, safe, dark, motionless, airless, it will change. It will not be broken; it will become unbreakable, impenetrable, irredeemable. . . . To love . . . is to be vulnerable.[5]

To Lewis's point, we wrap up our pain and hold on to it like a prize, refusing ever to set it down. It's a memorial to the madness we've faced and survived and a reminder to never let ourselves be played again.

But is that self-protection worth the cost of continuing to live isolated and sad?

For me, the answer is a hard no.

Recently, I reached out to Courtney. We hadn't talked in quite a while. I'd initially been shocked by how easily she'd cut me out of her life. She was that hurt. Given that reality, I figured a little space was best. But now I wanted to see if restoration might be possible. I wanted to apologize. I wanted to tell Courtney that I could now see what she saw so long ago and that I was working on it. I wanted to text again and try again and call each other friend again. We had been friends for more than a decade; would we really settle for never speaking again?

So I asked if we could meet. When she replied yes, I was so nervous that my heart raced.

I sat across from her, trembling and crying. She told me how I had hurt her and why she had pulled back. She told me things that were true, and I understood how hurt she must have been. She told me that she vividly remembered one time when I came over to her house and I cried and sat on her bed telling her my hurt. She said she'd never felt closer to me than she felt that day. But the rest of the time it was exhausting to be in a friendship where she was the only needy one. Like Jessica, my being a good friend to her meant my needing her. I wanted, and still I want, to get better at this. I apologized. She apologized.

Courtney forgave me and asked for forgiveness, and then we caught up on all we had missed. And I am so glad I braved opening the door again, a door I try to leave unlocked these days. Sometimes even cracked open, swinging lightly in the breeze. People run through it more and more, and I still wince a little when they intrude and make me say all the hard and face all the hard and deal with the hard. But sometimes they bring pizza or sushi, which makes it easier for me.

Even without bribes, I know that it's better this way. I am awkwardly learning.

This is the best way.

YOUR TURN

PRACTICE TRANSPARENT CONVERSATION

GRAB THE HANDFUL OF PEOPLE YOU'VE IDENTIFIED AS your three to five closest friends—or acquaintances with the potential to become close friends. Invite them to dinner this week and practice the six steps of having a vulnerable conversation.

If you're like me, you may have a difficult time being aware of what exactly is even happening inside you.

Some people will run from any deep conversation because they don't want to go there or they don't know how to go there. We have to get good at drawing people out. Here is an inventory to help chase down and (lovingly) tackle that friend who is running away from her feelings. (Written by someone who is an expert at running away from my hard feelings.)

To take some of the pressure off, you and your handful of friends can fill this out ahead of time and take turns reading your answers aloud during your time together:

This week at work (or at home) I was busy with _____ and I felt _____.

I think I felt that way because _____.

I wish that _____ would happen.

Very few people know that _____ is happening in my _____.

I need _____, but I am afraid to ask for it.

I am hesitant to open up because _____.

The greatest way you could love me right now is to

_____.

Ideas for Building Relationships with Transparency

· · · · · ·

- Instead of ordering something on Amazon, try to borrow it from your neighbor instead.
- Move your firepit or picnic table into the front yard. Talk to people as they walk by and invite them to join you!
- Invite your neighbors to watch a movie on a projector in your front yard.
- Ask your safe people to meet up for coffee and prepare them that you want to go deeper.
- Answer honestly the next time someone asks, "How are you doing?"
- Call a friend instead of texting her. Even if it's not a serious call, it gets you talking a little bit more.
- Ask your friends about the highs and lows of their week.
- Tell someone you like her. Literally say, "I like spending time with you."
- Work without your headphones. Make yourself available.
- Leave your phone in the car when you meet up with a friend.
- Ask someone for her advice with something you're struggling with, even if it's small.

BUT WHAT ABOUT . . .

. . . when I worry that what I shared is too much?

Start the conversation by saying, "I know this may be a little awkward, but I am new to this level of honesty and being vulnerable. Can you please be honest with me if I share too much too quickly? Your honesty will help me know how to share and grow in this."

If you really do this right, then at times you will share too much and sometimes you may get hurt by the response of others. That's okay. Sometimes people don't know what to do with difficulty. Give them grace and maybe slow down a little in how much you're sharing. But also don't assume you've overwhelmed them. Maybe they weren't sure how to respond but are incredibly grateful for how deep you just went. Remember, I told you this is a risk, and risky things feel uncomfortable. **The fact that it feels uncomfortable doesn't mean you're doing it wrong. In fact, it probably means you're doing it right.**

. . . if they repeatedly don't respond well to my vulnerability?

Absolutely, this will happen. I've warned you, so don't be surprised. This is part of the process of finding the right people. You risk sharing a little with someone and decide if it's safe to share a little more. Remember to be clear about how you need her to show up for you. Be sure to turn the tables and let her share as well.

Without a doubt, there are unsafe people. But part of finding the safe ones is risking and possibly being hurt by the unsafe ones.

. . . *the line between complaining and being vulnerable?*

Great question. Scripture says, "Do all things without grumbling or disputing, that you may be blameless and innocent, children of God without blemish in the midst of a crooked and twisted generation."[6] The apostle Paul, who penned those words, must have known that, while complaining feels good in the short term, it rarely solves the problem we're complaining about.

Complaining is usually centered on others rather than acknowledging our own role in the situation. Vulnerability, in comparison, requires humility and an eagerness to grow. Being truly (and appropriately) vulnerable begins with a heart that desires change, a heart that wants to break the bondage of a negative thought pattern and instead seek and walk in truth.

Complaining seeks relief. Vulnerability seeks transformation and connection.

I WANT OTHERS TO NEED
ME, BUT I DON'T WANT TO
HAVE TO NEED OTHERS.
—MAE ELIZABETH

PEOPLE DON'T
UNDERSTAND ME.
—KATY

I JUST CAN'T
SEEM TO AGREE WITH
PEOPLE. —MORGAN

I'M AFRAID IF I AM
VULNERABLE, I MIGHT
BE REJECTED. —SUE

I'M TOO MUCH FOR HER. —DANA

I DON'T WANT PEOPLE TO
JUDGE ME WHEN I LET MY
WALLS DOWN. —MEGAN

7.

PROTECTED

■

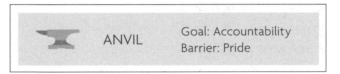

	ANVIL	Goal: Accountability Barrier: Pride

*S*EVERAL WEEKS AGO, LINDSEY, ASHLEY, CALLIE, AND MY NEW getting-closer-by-the-minute friend Jennie E. came over to the house. We chatted for a while, and then the conversation took a weird turn. I don't remember exactly what comment I made, but Ashley looked at me and said, "Jennie, it seems like you have a hard heart right now."

Ugh.

Ashley is not only my sister-in-law but my ask-the-hard-question, encourage-me-with-truth, pray-bolder-and-bigger prayers-than-I-am-comfortable-praying friend. And she's not afraid to tell it like it is. We all need an Ashley in our lives.

———

She had asked for an update about something sensitive, a struggle I was having in one of my relationships, and something about the way I'd answered sent a red flag flying high.

I sat there, stunned. "Really?" I said. "You're getting that from me?"

Lindsey chimed in. "I hate to say it, Jennie, but I agree."

I'm pretty sure I rolled my eyes at them as the following thoughts raced through my brain:

I'm fine.

Don't bug me right now.

I'm tired.

I just want to have fun.

Leave me alone.

This isn't a big deal.

I'm not the one who is wrong in this situation between that friend and me. Or I'm not that wrong. Maybe a little wrong but still, not in the mood.

Meanwhile, they continued to explain what they were sensing from me. "It feels like you're closed off somehow to your part in this whole thing," one of them said.

I was getting hot. I wasn't all that interested in going there, but *there* is exactly where we were going. "You're probably right," I said. "Honestly. I'm listening to what you're saying, and I probably have closed myself off to this situation."

My friends looked at me, silent for a moment. "Is that how you . . . *want* to be?" one of them finally asked with a smirk, knowing that I was writing this book.

What came next brought tears to my eyes, and my walled-off, hardened heart went soft. In the middle of our fun night together, they prayed for me and the situation. Later, as they each drove away, I smiled with raw cried-out eyes. I slept better that night than I had in days. I prayed better too. I lived freer, fuller, more at peace.

I am a professional heart hardener. I hate feeling pain, so I close myself off. These friends know this about me and love me anyway. Also, they love me too much to leave me there. They lasso me and pull me in, not only to themselves but to Jesus as well.

I hate it. And then I love it.

The Hard and the Beautiful
of Being Called Out

What is it about accountability that makes us squirm?

At its core, **accountability calls us to who we were meant to be,** through truth mixed with grace.

Yet our generation's declaration of personal independence has pushed this away.

We resent being challenged on our behavior.

But what if that missing element is exactly why we all feel like our relationships don't run deep?

I first met my friend Jey through some mutual friends. He is young and smart and joyful, and as he started filling in the blanks on his upbringing for me, I remember thinking, *It absolutely doesn't seem possible that this person and this story go together.*

Jey's childhood in the slums of Nairobi was rough. I mean, *rough* rough.

Rough, as in being born into generational poverty and forced to sell bootlegged liquor at age eight just to help keep the family afloat. Rough, as in waking up each day having no clue where his next meal was coming from, if there would even be a meal that day. Rough, as in being imprisoned at age nine for having stolen food that his single mom and siblings desperately needed to avoid utterly wasting away.

"When I was in prison," Jey told me, "I prayed to God for two things. I hadn't talked to Him before, but I sure was talking to Him now. So, the two requests: First, I wanted to get out of prison. And second, I wanted to get out of poverty. Which was just another form of prison, I guess."

Here's the funny thing about Jey: When you get him talking about his childhood, he smiles. He smiles a *lot*. He told me stories about the norm in Kenya of "holding each other's hands."

"Kids would show up at our little house because we didn't have doors or locks on our little hut," he said, "and my grandmother who lived with us would have no idea when they'd last eaten." She was barely keeping her own kids alive, you remember. But still, she'd usher those kids inside, she'd sit them at the table, and she'd feed them like they were her own.

He told me about how they shared. "There was no concept of 'mine,' or of privacy, or of ownership. Everything we had was ours."

Though Nairobi is a city of millions, within Jey's neighborhood his grandmother and others served as a village-sized community. He said, "I would be running on the other side of the slum, goofing off with friends, and would hear my name because 'the elders' were everywhere! And those elders would grab me by the collar right then and there and punish me, and, of course, my grandmother would hear about it."

Jey's life radically changed when in prison he got word that a family in the United States wanted to sponsor him through Compassion International, which meant that not only would he be freed from prison, but also that he and his siblings and mom would receive food, clean water, medical attention, and spiritual guidance each month, no thievery required. For the next decade, Jey worked hard in school and found work that eventually took him to the United States, where he lives now in Atlanta.

He'd spent a lifetime dreaming of getting to America, and now he was here. People weren't as destitute in Atlanta as in Nairobi, and Jey felt sure their abundance would make them even more open to the gospel. "When you aren't worried about food," he reasoned, "you can think about higher aims."

What Jey couldn't have anticipated was that, while life back in Kenya had been rough all those years, he'd enjoyed a type of prosperity that he didn't recognize until it was gone. "I miss the community, Jennie," he said. "Yeah, the people in my hometown were poor. But we were poor together." By contrast, in America, "everyone is very, very independent," Jey said. "They own their own houses, their own cars, their own lives."

When he spoke about what he missed about Nairobi, about the slums, he said, "I miss everyone being in and out of our lives. I wish that were true here. It's so different. I'm grateful for all we have here, but I wish my kids were growing up with tribal elders in their ears. I wish we could be part of a village here."

When we don't have a village of interconnected, consistent

teammates in our lives, we feel invisible, and **when we are left alone and unbothered, we become the worst version of ourselves.** Whether it is neighbors, or mentors, or grandparents, or our closest friends, we need people who see us. Who call us up and out.

But we hate words like . . .
    Submission.
            Accountability.
                Correction.

We find the idea of answering to others so uncomfortable that we want to run from it. What if we are running from what we most need—namely, to be caught? To be named, seen, noticed, and corrected is not the norm in our culture, but the Bible talks about it a lot:

- "If anyone is caught in any transgression, you who are spiritual should restore him in a spirit of gentleness."
- "Obey your leaders and submit to them, for they are keeping watch over your souls, as those who will have to give an account."
- "Let each one of you speak the truth with his neighbor, for we are members one of another."
- "If your brother sins against you, go and tell him his fault, between you and him alone. If he listens to you, you have gained your brother."
- "Without counsel plans fail, but with many advisers they succeed."

- "[Submit] to one another out of reverence for Christ."[1]

These are only a few of the dozens and dozens of Bible verses that speak to the importance of submission, accountability, and both receiving and giving loving correction.

The Benefits of Living Accountable

Our move to Dallas situated our home within a few blocks of extended family members, and our kids started attending school with their cousins. They were greeted at the school door on the first day by their grandfather, who works for the school and happens to be the famous and second winningest head football coach in Texas, which makes him something of a celebrity here. Being known as the grandkids of Coach Allen the minute they walked on campus was a huge asset at first. Everyone was nice to them, teachers had some context for who they were, and they reaped the benefits of the built-in favor that comes with such a relationship.

Then Kate slept through an important cross-country meeting, which, by team policy, meant she would not be allowed to participate in the next meet. She came home ghost white with fear and told us what had happened. Looking up from her puddle of shame, she said, "Now I have to tell Coach."

That's what all the grandkids call their grandad—Coach.

I smiled, and she cried. Am I cruel? Not at all. I just recognize the benefits of living accountable. My kids now have a new layer of accountability in their lives. No longer are they just answering to Mom and Dad, but they also have to face their grandparents and their aunt and uncle, who live across the street from the school and also keep tabs on them now.

Accountability Makes Us More Effective

"As iron sharpens iron," Proverbs says, "so one person sharpens another."[2] Iron on iron: the symbolism is taken from the ancient process that still happens in my kitchen today. Whenever a knife (or sword, if that's your thing) gets dull, you run it across another sharp metal surface, and soon two useless dull pieces of metal become useful sharpening tools, each one refined by the other for mutual good.

I lost my knife sharpener for years and finally picked one up recently. I had no idea how dull and ineffective my knives had become until I vigorously pulled their blades against that metal rod and then sliced through a tomato.

It flew through the tomato in one slash. My jaw dropped. My knife was so happy! It was finally serving its purpose again! Why had I left it sitting there, dull, boring, and inefficient for so long? It was meant to be sharp.

When you add accountability to the necessary proximity and transparency we've addressed, you unleash a new level of potency in your life. You grow sharper, more effective. You change. As we will talk about in the next chapter, healthy relationships thrive when they are connected to a shared mission and purpose. But if you skip this practice of accountability, you miss the whole point. You miss being sharpened and made more effective for that purpose.

The solution?

Choose friends who have the potential to make you better. Then allow them to do just that.

Accountability Calls Us to Live Better

This might be the most radical thing I've said so far: all over the world and in all other generations, living a life of accountability is considered not the exception but the rule. It's the thing Jey missed about living in Kenya—someone to catch him. And someone to catch his daughters, to love them enough to help them become the best possible version of themselves.

If you are a follower of Christ, your new self longs to be caught. We aren't comfortable in our sin. We are a "new creation," remember? "Therefore, if anyone is in Christ, he is a new creation. The old has passed away; behold, the new has come."[3]

And when our old selves are gone, we are never again at home in our sin.

We were wired to live in the light, to be known, seen, and challenged to live better lives.

When I recently took Cooper back to Rwanda for over a week, his aunties and surrogate tribal elders took it upon themselves to parent him. Auntie Alice and Pastor Fred were always with us and always correcting him and instructing him, teaching him, exhorting him to be his best.

When Cooper was showing off to a slew of street kids who were visibly impressed with him, Pastor Fred pulled him aside, knelt in front of him, and put his hands on my kid's shoulders. Gently he said, "Cooper, you are missing a great opportunity to ask these boys questions about their lives too. I know it feels good to be treated as though you are special, but these children are special as well. You have a responsibility to see them and to take an interest in them, just as Jesus would do, to show that you know how to engage with them, and listen to them, and care."

My jaw dropped. I hadn't asked Pastor Fred to coparent with me that week. He was just doing what *everyone* in his culture does. Believers in Rwanda collaborate, holding each other and anyone they love to the standard of Jesus and letting them know when they fall short. Whether aunties and uncles by blood or by choice, accountability is the language of village life.

Accountability Challenges Us to Reach Higher

Accountability isn't just about sin avoidance or sin mitigation. It's about challenging and inspiring one another, telling a friend she's underestimating her abilities or urging her to take a risk when you see her holding back instead of dreaming big for God.

While writing this morning, I got in a conversation with the two young girls seated at the table next to me, who were eating brunch together. They told me that they met today to dream about the new year. I was familiar with the light in their eyes and the notes they were taking as they talked. I knew those happy tears, shed over eggs and thick slices of bacon. I recognized what they were doing. They were choosing to get better together.

Bacon, coffee, dreams, making each other better, believing for each other what is difficult to believe for ourselves, reminding each other of Jesus and grace and heaven—this is the good stuff of friendships that will last.

The Process of Being Sharpened

I'm often asked about what I think makes friendships work, about what I think authentic community is, and while there are several aspects to that vision, at the top of the list would be the practice of saying hard things and the practice of listening to and receiving those hard things.

"As iron sharpens iron, so one person sharpens another," remember? We have the opportunity to both sharpen and be sharpened, if only we'll see our relationships as the anvil that they are. And yet who in a right mind wants to sign up for being the piece of metal that's getting reshaped? Torturous flames, the pounding against an unforgiving surface, the bending and prodding and pain. Nobody thinks they want that experience, but we do. We actually crave it. We just don't always know how to have it.

Begin with answering this: *Who in your life has wisdom to speak into your life?*

Maybe it is a peer or somebody older. Remember that village life includes friends and mentors and a wider net of people who can speak wisdom into your life, not just your obvious two to three closest.

Once you've identified your wise and trustworthy friend or friends, here's how you intentionally pursue accountability:

1. Give permission to this person or people to tell the truth to you.
2. Ask them regularly:

   a. *What area do you see in my life that I need to grow in?*
   b. *What practices do I need to embrace in order to grow and mature?*
   c. *Will you hold me accountable to this change?*

3. Plan a follow-up meeting. Schedule a time when you can revisit this conversation.
4. Ask your friend or friends if you can hold them accountable for anything.

Don't Settle for Nice

Listen, because this is important: ***don't take criticism from just anyone.*** Choose the voices you intend to listen to. Give permission to only certain people to speak truth into your life. Look for people who will call you up higher, not those who will let things slide.

I've noticed a trend that suggests we must prioritize acceptance and tolerance at all costs, regardless of the decisions people are making, the behaviors they're manifesting, the beliefs they're clinging to, or any of a thousand other things that may be leading them into harm. If we listen to what society tells us, then we will put tolerance at the tip-top of the list of requirements to be a good friend.

To each her own.
  Honor your truth.
  You do you.

It's all nonsense. Why? Because the last thing you and I need are friends who do nothing more than cosign our stupidity. If I'm about to career off a cliff and you choose to stand there cheering for me, we've got a problem. I don't need acceptance when I'm being a fool; I need help. And so do you.

Don't Surround Yourself with Mirrors

We not only need people who call out our foolishness, we need people in our lives who are not carbon copies of ourselves. We need to be in community with people of differing ethnicities, backgrounds, perspectives. As I've watched the Church become so divided in the past few years, I have leaned more deeply into relationships with people who think differently, who call out, for example, how an ideology impacts my friends of color. It's one thing to watch the news and form an opinion about a policy. It is altogether a different thing to sit across from a friend who is teary about how to raise her child of color in a world fixated on hate.

We need people who challenge our presuppositions, increase our compassion, call out our racism, and challenge our materialism. So often those people have lives wildly different from mine. Sure, they love Jesus, but they have experienced the world and see it in ways I grow from and respect. It's why my family loves to travel and counts handfuls of friends in many countries. We realize that our little spot on planet Earth, the color of our skin, the privilege we carry from parents who own homes and have secure incomes, the church we attend, the level of education we received—all this has shaped our opinions and perspectives.

How will we ever have our wrong thinking challenged or small thinking expanded without friends to challenge and expand it?

The Great Cover-Up

But we face a bigger enemy than discomfort when it comes to living accountable: our pride.

If shame makes us hide behind locked doors and high walls, pride is the paint, the wreath, and the cute landscaping that says, "All good here! In fact, we are better than good. We are amazing! Look at our beautiful new shrubs."

Pride is the great cover-up for the fact that we are all sinners, in need of grace.

Adam and Eve eat the fruit, hide from God, and then devise a plan. *Maybe He won't notice we're naked and ashamed if we put on these cute little leaves?* So they pull out their sewing machine, throw together little outfits, and come out of hiding with their heads held high.

———

"All good here!" they chime. But God knows better.

Adam blames Eve.

Eve blames the snake.

Pride sinks them both.

Pride is our defense when we are accused. Pride is our insistence that our opinion is Bible truth. Pride is our good works we set out to showcase our virtue. Our achievements that affirm we are justified in our choices. Our proof we wave around to show we aren't sinful.

But nothing on earth is more freeing than just owning our mistakes.

Being caught.

Admitting we sin.

Laying down our defenses and resting in God's provision for our sins.

People who live this way are my favorites! They are self-deprecating and never defensive; they're fun and honest and free.

I have Tim Keller in my earbuds so often that I've practically memorized most of his sermons, and one of my favorite takeaways from his body of work is this:

———

Our sin is worse than we imagine.

And the grace of God is bigger and better than we can imagine.

Accepting both truths sets us free.

A friend was griping to me about her mother-in-law a few days ago and got herself so worked up that she was almost in tears—angry tears. I watched as she tried to collect herself, and it was as if a giant neon sign appeared over her head flashing the word *fear . . . fear . . . fear.*

"What are you afraid of?" I asked in almost a whisper, once she'd moved through the emotional burst.

The griping stopped, and the conversation turned to what was *really* going on.

I just said what I saw. I didn't shame her for griping or for being afraid. I just observed aloud what she couldn't see for herself, and she was able to safely process the true problem she needed to address in herself and in her expectations. I didn't let her spin in her anger and rage. I didn't leave her there, because leaving isn't love.

I'm not going to lie: practicing two-way accountability is messy, and we sometimes clumsily hurt others more than we help. But if we just laid down our defensive posture and listened and learned, then maybe we'd find something better waiting for us. True accountability comes from deep love and care for our people. If our people know we love them, we can bear with one another when our words come out a little wrong. We love them too much to leave them.

Often, we run when it gets difficult, but what if we stayed and didn't cover up? What if the hard stuff is what brings the depth of friendship we are craving?

Yes, when we set aside our fig leaves and say what is true, or when we hear and listen to what is true, we put ourselves at greater risk of being hurt. I know. No one has wounded me more than the people who are closest to me. And sometimes my imperfect people speak harm and not correction. Sometimes they don't understand or empathize. Sometimes they use my sin against me. Sometimes they gossip about what I have shared. Sometimes they leave me in judgment. Sometimes they reject me because I was honest. Sometimes they shut me out for good.

To be perfectly candid, these realities are terrifying. But even though every one of the things I just named has happened to me personally, I'm still pleading with you to sign up for this way of life. And I'm telling myself the same thing.

Here's the deal: If you're committed to grow in maturity and increase in wisdom and be relationally healthier ten years from now than you are at this moment, then you will start to see that iron anvil I mentioned not as punishment but as a means to the progress you desperately need. You will quit hiding, hedging, and decorating your wreath for your locked door. You will stop recoiling when questions are asked. You will give up on pretending that you have it all together. You will let a little useful pounding into your life.

Why? Because Scripture says we need this: "Exhort one another every day, as long as it is called 'today,' that none of you may be hardened by the deceitfulness of sin."[4]

Lay It All Out There

God's way to protect us from the enemy and sin is to share responsibility with each other—our people fighting for us and us fighting for them.

I've seen this. Often. In our small group, we go *deep*. I mean, we show each other all of it. And yet I have never experienced a group of people fight for us as this group does.

Since our earliest days in Dallas more than three years ago, Zac and I have been in this small group I've told you about, a weekly gathering of couples, organized through our church. I had no other friends in town, as you'll recall, so I said yes to the invitation to join, despite my serious reservations.

A few months in, the leader matter-of-factly said something like, "Next week we're going to lay out our finances for each other, including numbers, and talk about how we can hold each other accountable in our generosity, spending, and debt."

Wait, I remember thinking. *You want to know what?!*

Yep. They wanted specifics on purchases being considered, purchases that had been made, and overall financial standing. They wanted data—as in, spreadsheets were encouraged.

One of the couples was in the market for a new house, so, as was the custom of this group, they brought all the information to the other couples—how much the house would cost, how much they planned to use as a down payment and how much cash that would leave on hand, what the annual taxes and other fees would be on this new living situation, other major expenses they were facing (not the least of which was two kids soon to be in college), and so forth. And then a massive conversation ensued.

People asked questions. People made observations. People offered alternatives for consideration. People prayed for clarity and wisdom on behalf of the prospective homebuyers. And as I sat there taking in all this activity, something almost tangible fell away from me. Fear fell. Because I saw how beautiful and reassuring accountability could be.

Since then, for the past four years, Zac and I have run every major financial decision by our group. And while that may sound horrifying to you—"You tell them everything?"—it has been a tremendous source of peace in our lives, this knowledge that these fellow sojourners have our backs. "Plans fail for lack of counsel," Proverbs says, "but with many advisers they succeed."[5] I'd always nodded in agreement with that sentiment; now I was doing what it says to do.

"But doesn't that information ever get used against you?" you ask.

I suppose it could someday. Weaponization is always possible, but so far the benefits have outweighed the risks.

If accountability is done right and with the right people, we will love Jesus more and our lives will show that love to be real.

Setting the Ground Rules

I feel compelled to note that it's way too easy to do this all wrong. When you sit across from someone and you share your struggles and they share theirs, the natural inclination is to solve each other's problems rather than point each other to Christ. We may be able to put a Band-Aid on each other's issues, but what if we pointed our friends to the ultimate Physician instead of our quick fixes? Going to Jesus is where you start to see supernatural life change.

The first Bible study I wrote was called *Stuck: The Places We Get Stuck and the God Who Sets Us Free.* I taught this study for the first time in my home church because I knew I needed it and my friends needed it. About 150 women of all different ages came and sat in a little cafeteria of our church plant. We used conversation cards to guide the discussion, and the whole time, whenever we asked a really deep question, we ended up counseling each other. The women would tell each other how they handled situations from their own experience instead of pointing to the Word of God.

After that, I completely rebuilt the way I did Bible study. I set ground rules. I put Scripture at the center. At the beginning of each small group gathering, even if you had been in it four or five times, you had to read the ground rules together. The ground rules remain: **We don't counsel each other with human wisdom. We point to the Word of God.**

When one person shares a concern, another responds, "Okay, I hear you. Now, let's go hear from God." We don't stop with venting. We don't stop with fix-it worldly wisdom. We take all of it together to God and His Word.

You and I need friends who, instead of trying to fix us, help us to fix our eyes more firmly on Jesus.

The Safest Place

In Rwanda, Pastor Fred called up Cooper to a different way of engaging with those village boys, a way that would not just stroke Coop's ego, but that would honor each person present. In that moment, Cooper had a decision to make. He could either push back against that input—whether silently, by fuming, or verbally, by pleading his case—or he could receive the feedback and improve.

I have to give props to my son, who chose the better way. He listened to Pastor Fred's advice, then he acted on it. As in, right then and there, he did. He course corrected in the moment, and his entire day changed as a result.

Our group left that village and headed to the next stop, about an hour's van ride away. After the initial hustle and bustle of loading up, hollering goodbye, and sticking arms out the windows to wave at our new friends until they were mere specks in the dust cloud we'd kicked up, a quiet settled over the lot of us. We were filled up and worn out and spent.

I peeked at Cooper, who was nestled into the last row of the van, to check on him, to smile at him. And the image I saw I will never forget: Cooper's head was leaning on Pastor Fred's shoulder and Pastor Fred's head was resting on Cooper's head. My boy and Pastor Fred were both fast asleep.

We want this kind of accountability. We find rest in it. Truth in love is the safest place to be, even if it stings a little. Iron sharpens iron. It isn't supposed to be comfortable. But it leads us closer to God and closer to who He wants us to be—and that ends up feeling like home.

YOUR TURN

PURSUE ACCOUNTABILITY TOGETHER

—

BEFORE YOU MEET WITH YOUR FRIENDS THIS WEEK, SPEND some time reflecting on the following questions and writing your answers in your journal or making notes in your phone:

WHAT'S GOING ON?

Why am I worried?

What problems am I facing?

Where am I feeling insecure?

What sin am I fighting?

What am I learning?

What am I trying to control?

Then when you gather with your friends, discuss your answers to these questions. Share a problem you're facing and ask your group to speak into it or help solve it. Make a plan together and take time praying about what each of you shared.

Ideas for Finding Accountability

· · · · · ·

- Ask people for advice. This opens up room for them to speak candidly.
- Remember what your friend tells you. Put prompts on your calendar or in your phone to remind you to pray.
- Do an overnight retreat with five friends you are getting close with.
- Give a few trusted people permission to call you out.
- Get around older women and ask them to show you how to handle a situation.
- Look for someone approximately fifteen years older than you. Ask her, "What's one piece of advice you'd give yourself if you were in the same season I'm in?"

BUT WHAT ABOUT . . .

. . . *when I address sin in a friend's life and she doesn't receive it well?*

I'm a big believer in asking permission in friendships. Ask, "Do you want to hold each other accountable to growing and maturing? I would love for you to speak into my life, and I would love to speak into your life, if you agree."

Some people will reject the invitation and some people will crave it and some people will take it but the conversation will be so uncomfortable you'll think you shouldn't have done it. That's okay. If they give you permission, stay the course.

However, many people overuse the verse "As for those who persist in sin, rebuke them in the presence of all, so that the rest may stand in fear" and underuse the verse "Why do you see the speck that is in your brother's eye, but do not notice the log that is in your own eye?"[6] So let's be slow to call out other people's sin, while being quick to ask them to call out our sin.

. . . *determining if someone is a trustworthy voice in my life?*

First, look for healthy people and become a healthy person. Counselor Jim Cofield shared with me once some basic qualities of a healthy friend.[7] Ready?

- I am a receptive person rather than reactive.
- I am more resilient than rigid.

- I am aware and mindful rather than unaware and emotionally clueless.
- I am responsible for my own life.
- I don't blame or take victim status.
- I am empathetic.
- I am strong.
- I am stable.
- I am realistic.
- I don't have expectations that are unattainable.
- I see the world in a beautiful way and don't grow stale.
- I believe God is for me.
- I am grateful and content.
- I know how to trust, hope, be humble, desire, and love well.

. . . knowing how long to be friends with someone before I invite her to speak into my life?

To some degree, no matter how long you have known someone, it will feel like a risk. No one is perfectly safe. Trust builds as you share vulnerably in smaller ways. But when you have seen enough to believe this is someone you enjoy and you want to attempt to trust, go for it!

I'M TOO EXHAUSTED
FROM BEING A MOM, WIFE,
EMPLOYEE TO BE
A GOOD FRIEND. —KENNEDY

THE THING THAT STOPS ME
FROM FINDING AND KEEPING MY
PEOPLE IS THAT I WORRY THAT
THEY WILL TAKE ME AWAY FROM
MY FIRST PRIORITIES: MY FAMILY
AND MINISTRY. —STELA H.

NOBODY IS
AVAILABLE
WHEN I NEED
THEM. —TERI

I DON'T KNOW HOW TO GET
PAST THE GETTING-TO-
KNOW-YOU SMALL TALK.
—EMILY

TO BE HONEST, IT'S
EASIER TO DO LIFE BY
MYSELF. —ASHLEY

PEOPLE DON'T
HAVE TIME
FOR ME. —JOY

8.

DEEP

■

	SHOVEL	Goal: Shared Purpose Barrier: Shallow/Small Talk

WHAT'S KEEPING YOU BUSY THESE DAYS? WHAT ARE YOU UP to today, this week? I'm serious. What activities are you involved in? Not what are you thinking about doing, or what are you thinking about becoming involved in, but rather, what are you actually doing? What responsibilities are you carrying week to week during this particular season of life? What roles are you playing? What things are you expected to show up for? Where are you investing your time and heart?

More important, as you think about all the places you go in a given week, who do you see beside you? Take a look at the chart we created in chapter 6.

During the pandemic, a friend was lamenting the isolation she felt due to what seemed to be a never-ending series of lockdowns and restrictions. I totally got her frustration. But I also knew that some parts of life were still happening for her, even if on a modified or reduced scale.

"What is still happening?" I asked her. "Take this past week, for example. What things were you able to do?"

Turns out her elementary-age kids were still in school. And her daughter's dance classes were still held. And her six-person book club still met outdoors. She'd run errands almost every day. She'd been in countless Zoom meetings because she and her colleagues were still working from home. She'd spent an afternoon serving a nonprofit she's part of, packing holiday care packages for women and men who would spend Thanksgiving and Christmas in the prison south of town.

"I know you haven't been able to do everything you want to do lately, but your last seven days sound pretty amazing!" I told her. "You were around tons of people. Why not strike up a friendship with them?"

My friend's involvements during this season of her life, the activities that required her to show up, in the flesh, and engage, included such variety: work meetings, kid's dance class, errands, volunteer work, book club, and more. Yet even with all these encounters with other people who were doing the same things she was doing—accomplishing meaningful work, keeping a busy household running, reading good books, and so forth—my friend felt isolated and alone. Why? Because her closest friends weren't involved in any of those aspects of her life. It's as if her people and her priorities existed in separate worlds.

Why Our Lives Feel
Fractured and Disconnected

It may be difficult to imagine, but there was a time in history when a person's life work happened solely and completely in the context of the community he called home. The appropriately named Fertile Crescent, an area that includes such modern-day locales as Syria, Iraq, Jordan, and Israel, is thought to have been the site of the first recognized practice of agriculture. Entire bands of hunter-gatherers stopped roaming and settled down there thousands of years ago. They learned to make tools. They learned to domesticate plants and animals. They learned to construct more permanent housing. They learned to create something of a stable existence for themselves.[1]

And just as important as what they were doing was who they were doing it with: the other people who lived there too. Yes, these communities worked together, but they also ate meals together and relaxed together at the end of the day. They raised children together and solved problems together and lived the entirety of their lives in plain view of others in their midst.

But during the Industrial Revolution people started to choose better jobs over the communities, the *people*, they loved. People started working in factories in cities, which generally meant that instead of sticking around to work the family farm young people moved away to the city, reducing time spent with family and friends. Where once the sun set the pace for working life, now people logged twelve-hour days, if not longer.

Through the nineteenth century as cities grew and housing became more difficult to find, many people spent additional hours riding the train home to the suburbs after long workdays.

They weren't people "of" the city, just people who worked there. At the same time, they spent less and less time at home and in their neighborhoods. Soon enough, both places lacked community, connection, anything more than superficial interaction.

No wonder loneliness showed up.

From there, the suburbanization of the entire Western world rolled like a wave through society, further separating family from family, person from person, soul from soul, life from life. Add to that trend the recent emergence of social media, which elevates virtual connection over all that happens in real life, and it's pretty easy to see why so many people feel so isolated.

Our work lives have little to do with our home lives.
  Our home lives have little to do with our social lives.
  Our social lives have little to do with our spiritual lives—if we still have spiritual lives at all.

It's as if we're trying to live simultaneously in three separate realities. No wonder we're exhausted and frazzled. We're running in fifteen different directions day by day, bumping into scores of people, even as we feel utterly alone. Then we spend our spare minutes scrolling Instagram, where everyone looks perfectly connected and happy, or scrolling the news, where we pick up a fresh batch of problems we are supposed to be caring about and tweeting about and crafting a plan to solve.

  Any attempts to carve out time to love others and connect with others just add to the pressure and busyness we already carry, and so we isolate even further.

This chaos is too much for our minds to carry.

But what if I gave you permission to simplify? What if already built into your schedule was a team waiting to run with you, people ready to be something deeper than supper club friends, individuals who could be your teammates through blood, sweat, and tears?

A Bigger Vision for Relationship

Let me ask you this:

Who could you pull into the missions you are already accomplishing?

Who could you join on their missions?

Who are you already on mission with that could become a deeper friend?

Throughout so much of history—and still today, in two-thirds of the world's countries—people have lived in the context of a tight-knit community, whether a village, a people group, a tribe. And those groups historically are unified around a shared purpose. Every person has a role. Some roles are hands-on: there are people who hunt, people who tend crops, people who cook, people who serve. Some roles are leadership based: there are chiefs and song leaders and child-rearers and scribes. Some people are better than others at seeing problems. Some people are better than others at solving problems. Some villagers are funny. Some are compassionate. Some are artistic. Some are wise. But no role is more important than another. It takes everyone to make the thing work.

This type of system likely sounds familiar to you, because it's written into the very fiber of your design as a human being. Long before humankind tamed the Fertile Crescent, God Himself laid out a community with a shared mission, as you'll recall. To Adam and Eve He said, "Be fruitful and increase in number; fill the earth and subdue it. Rule over the fish in the sea and the birds in the sky and over every living creature that moves on the ground."[2] To the disciples Jesus said as He was going to heaven, "Go make more disciples." To the local church God's plan again was spelled out by the apostle Paul: "For just as each of us has one body with many members," we read in Romans 12, "and these members do not all have the same function, so in Christ we, though many, form one body, and each member belongs to all the others."[3]

God gives the people who follow Him a shared purpose, along with gifts that require us to depend on each other to accomplish that purpose.

We all crave being connected in a shared purpose because we all were built for it.

You want to know one of the biggest problems we face when it comes to friendship? **We mistakenly think friendship is about us.**

But the most satisfying and bonding types of relationships arise when friendship and community are centered on a bigger mission. And guess what? If you're a follower of Jesus, then:

1. You have a built-in mission no matter your job, neighborhood, hobby, club, or school: share the love of God.

2. You have a village, a team, to pursue that mission
with you: your local church.

**As members of the body of Christ, we are to love each
other and God so well that other people want this love and
follow Jesus.**

We read in the gospel of Luke that Jesus sent out seventy-two
disciples in pairs with the assignment to just love people, eat
with people, and be with people. Then they were to report
back on whether each village was a good place to minister. He
never sent people alone, and He always began ministry with
sharing food and spending time in homes, *in relationship.*

I mentioned earlier that I'm privileged to lead a nonprofit
organization called IF:Gathering. We build tools and experiences to help women connect with God. Our team feels more
like a family than coworkers, evidenced at this moment by the
endless text thread we're all on, where one of us keeps posting
new-baby pictures and another is asking for prayer for a dead-
line. We do life together in deep ways. We call out each other's
sin. We share meals, even when the gatherings have nothing
to do with work. My kids count many of my longtime teammates at IF:Gathering as aunties and friends. **We do life together.**

I always tell my team that how we love God and each
other is the most important work we do in this office. Something about that is foreign to our concept of work in America.
But we are bound together in a shared mission and a calling
that defines our relationships more profoundly than any title
or salary or org chart. We run after God together, and we help

other people do the same. It's sacred work, and it is a mission that unites us in a deeper way than just sharing an office and accomplishing a task.

One of my earliest teammates is Chloe Hamaker. Chloe and I started working together long distance more than seven years ago, when I was just beginning public ministry. She eventually ended up taking over much of my ministry as the executive director.

Two years ago, I was at a birthday party for my sister Brooke, who runs a dude ranch in Colorado and lives intimately connected to a lot of her coworkers. At the party were amazing women of various ages, all of whom invest in my sister and whom my sister counts as dear friends. Yes, technically they work for Brooke, but as I watched them interact I realized that my sister does not have a dividing line between work and life. These are her friends, and they are on mission together each day.

Later that night, just past 11:00 p.m., I picked up my phone to call Chloe.

She answered, surprised that I was calling so late.

"I need to tell you something," I blurted. "You are one of my best friends! I know that sounds really awkward since we've been friends for more than seven years, and I don't know if that crosses some work-life boundary, but through working together for all these years, you really have become one of my very best friends."

Chloe laughed and said, "Well, I know."

Even though she is more than ten years my junior and is in a different life stage than I am and reports to me on an org chart, she had long gotten used to the idea that we were the dearest of sister-friends. We go to each other's birthdays and talk on the phone so much that Siri made her my emergency contact. Don't worry—Zac is one too. But having a shared mission and doing life together really does make two people the *closest* of friends.

Go Do Something—Together

C. S. Lewis said, "Friendship must be about something, even if it were only an enthusiasm for dominoes or white mice. Those who have nothing can share nothing; those who are going nowhere can have no fellow-travellers."[4]

Whether you attend school or manage a home or manage a company, work was meant to bring fulfillment and promote thriving for those we love and know. But we complain about our God-given jobs, and we gossip about the God-given people we've been given to do that work beside. Worse, work has been redefined as a hollow pursuit of money rather than a pursuit of human thriving. This is *so* not the point!

My favorite podcast pastor, Tim Keller, said it this way:

[Work] is rearranging the raw material of God's creation in such a way that it helps the world in general, and people in particular, thrive and flourish.

This pattern is found in all kinds of work. Farming takes the physical material of soil and seed and produces food. Music takes the physics of sound and rearranges it into something beautiful and thrilling that brings meaning to life. When we take fabric and make a piece of clothing, when we push a broom and clean up a room, when we use technology to harness the forces of electricity, when we take an unformed, naive human mind and teach it a subject, when we teach a couple how to resolve their relational disputes, when we take simple materials and turn them into a poignant work of art—we are continuing God's work of forming, filling, and subduing. Whenever we bring order out of chaos, whenever we draw out creative potential, whenever we elaborate and "unfold" creation beyond where it was when we found it, we are following God's pattern of creative cultural development.[5]

So we start with a mission to bring thriving and then we look for colaborers to build with. It is the greatest and messiest fun!

Maybe your days are filled with toddlers or college classes or PTA task lists. Fine. But what if those places became mission fields and the people in your places became teammates? Don't you want to be part of something exciting and meaningful? Are you sick of living in your bubble of self-fulfillment and meeting your own small needs? What if you got to wake up every day with an assignment and a team of people by your side?

You can. This one truly is as simple as a change in perspective.

My friend Pete told me about when his father-in-law fell ill and had to move to a nursing home. This elderly man of God felt frustrated that he could no longer minister to people the way he had for so many decades. But instead of giving up, he decided that if he was going to be bedridden in a nursing home and unable to go anywhere, then that room would have to be where he did his work and the nursing staff would have to be his team!

"He had us make a sign to hang on his door," Pete said. It read:

House of Forgiveness

MARVIN W. BURNHAM

Every single day, from the time he moved in until the day he passed away, people would knock on that door, slip inside, sit down in the guest chair that was pulled up close to his bed, and confide in him their disappointments in life, both the sins that had been done against them and the sins that they themselves had committed. In response, Mr. Burnham would hold their hands, nod his head in understanding, and speak words that healed their souls. "If you will accept it, Jesus wants to forgive you," he would say. "And when you have been forgiven, you can go and forgive others too."

Mr. Burnham's funeral was one big lovefest, a celebration of the sneaky ways the staff helped him run his little operation and the lives changed by it.

Anywhere can become a place to carry out your mission and anyone can become teammates.

Don't sit on your rear end at home and try to make friends. Go do something. Teach Sunday school, volunteer at VBS, join a kickball team. What is something you can commit to for six months? *That.* Go do that and find some people to do it with you. Or choose to see the potential friendships right under your nose in the activities you're already pursuing.

Friends won't fall from the sky. Friends are always *made.*

We Are Gathered Together to Give Love Away

It bears repeating: if you are a follower of Jesus, you truly do have a significant purpose attached to every seemingly mundane part of your life. There is a weight to every human we see on the street, at the playground, at the store, in your apartment complex.

C. S. Lewis said it this way: "There are no *ordinary* people. You have never talked to a mere mortal. Nations, cultures, arts, civilizations—these are mortal, and their life is to ours as the life of a gnat. But it is immortals whom we joke with, work with, marry, snub, and exploit—immortal horrors or everlasting splendours."[6]

We carry weighty purpose into every interaction we have, and every human carries in them a weight of glory. When we understand this idea, we love differently. We view our daily work and encounters differently.

A friend who is a pastor in the underground church told me, "We have a saying in the Middle East that you don't know someone until you've gone on a trip with them and you've eaten with them. It's so true. The camaraderie. You don't see that in the West. When, for example, COVID-19 hit the Middle East, me and the leaders all hunkered down in one house. The twenty of us with kids. You really bond when that happens."

He continued, "True discipleship doesn't happen out there; it happens in a home. **True discipleship isn't something you do once a week. It's what you do every day because that's when you get to know people.** It's when you're with them during the good times and the bad times. When they're sick and when they're healthy. That's what builds true family. The blood of Christ makes us family, but we need to experience it together every day."

On mission together. Making disciples in our ordinary moments.

God built a longing inside each of us to be about something other than our own individual success. We're going to be in heaven together forever with the people we love, so our goal in connecting isn't just personal satisfaction, but to see people saved before Jesus returns.

If you want good friends, then run a race together, build a house together, cook a meal together, and do it all while working together for the greatest mission a human can have: giving God away.

It isn't good for anyone to be alone and also isn't good for man (or woman) to be idle! In the beginning and before the Fall, God gave us each other and then He gave us actual real-life, get-your-hands-dirty work to do.

Alone we want to escape or cope, but in community we help each other do hard things.

I am about to get up in your business—or God's Word is, anyway. Here is what the apostle Paul said in 2 Thessalonians:

"We hear that some among you walk in idleness, not busy at work, but busybodies. Now such persons we command and encourage in the Lord Jesus Christ to do their work."[7]

In other words? *Get busy!*

I asked my pastor friend why the Church in the West has lost the sense of camaraderie and connectedness that characterizes his community in the Middle East. He said, "Because the West is all about individualism, convenience, and being comfortable. **Discipleship is inconvenient, uncomfortable, and very messy.**"

My friend Ann said it this way: "I want to die working beside people I love with dirt under my fingernails." Dirt under our fingernails, building a garden that goes on forever. Not a bad way to live.

Let's get back to the simple way of following Jesus and making disciples. It doesn't have to be complicated. Just tell somebody about your God. Choose the line with the cashier instead of the self-checkout line, look her in the eyes, and talk with her. Put family and people back in your everyday life. And together fight back against this individualistic culture that has intoxicated us into thinking that convenience and personal achievement equal happiness, because they don't.

Our time on earth is short.

Our mission is crucial.

We have to get back to building the kingdom, messily, dirt under our fingernails—together.

YOUR TURN

FINDING A WAY TO SERVE TOGETHER

—

FIRST, A QUICK ASSESSMENT. THERE ARE 168 HOURS IN A week. Let's take inventory of how you are spending time.

ACTIVITY

TIME SPENT

_____   _____hours

_____   _____hours

_____   _____hours

_____   _____hours

_____   _____hours

_____   _____hours

_____   _____hours

_____   _____hours

In view of your God-given purpose to love others into eternity, what does this list reveal about where you need to:

1. Add (Do you have a significant amount of margin?)

    ____

2. Subtract (Are you too busy for people?)

    ____

3. Invite + Include (How can you intentionally build your close friends and purposeful interactions into your week?)

Hopefully you're building traction with a few people you want to continue on with. Or maybe you still don't see a lot of potential. If so, you might invite new friends to join you in a specific activity. Either way, put yourself out there with a few people and trust the process.

Ideas for Pursuing a Mission Together

· · · · · ·

- Join a club. Gardening, tennis, cards, running, biking, volunteering.
- Go play pickleball, tennis, spikeball. Invite the people on the court to join your game.

- Host a freezer meal night. Chop and prepare the food together and everyone takes home a few meals!
- As a small group, sign up for a semester of kids' ministry duty together, working in the nursery, teaching a class, mentoring teens.
- Go to fun workout classes. Struggle together, laugh, and get Sonic afterward!
- Plan a supper club with your neighbors. Cook through a cookbook together! Everyone prepares and brings one recipe.
- Paint someone's room, clean out a closet, or plant some flowers together.
- If you usually work at home by yourself, take your laptop to a coffee shop one morning and invite a friend to sit with you.

BUT WHAT ABOUT . . .

. . . if I just don't have time for this?

I realize that few people are sitting around looking for more to do. But take another look at your time inventory. Are you doing the things that will give purpose and meaning to the most important parts of life, such as relationships and connection? Make sure you're doing the right things with your time. If you're truly busy, there should be opportunities already baked into your life to connect more deeply with people. You just have to view them that way.

... taking a relationship deeper when we
already spend a lot of time together?

Have a dreaming session, lay out some of the ideas above, and choose one to try. Not all of them. Just pick one simple way to connect over a shared mission that incorporates your mutual passions and gifts.

... the fact that I'm single and all my married
friends are always busy with their spouses
or kids? How do I do this if they're too busy
for me?

Some of my very best friends are single, and I appreciate that they are more flexible about dropping by and running errands with me. Initiate with your friends who have kids. Chances are, they'll be grateful for adult conversation and companionship. People still get lonely and in a rut once they have a spouse or a family. And your friendship is still needed in their lives. Be sure to ask them to keep initiating with you too. Tell them you are comfortable being invited to be a part of their family.

RIGHT WHEN I START TO GET
DEEP WITH SOMEONE, I PULL
BACK WHEN THERE'S A HINT
OF TENSION OR I THINK THEY
MIGHT BE UPSET WITH ME.
—BROOKE

I HAVE EXPECTATIONS
OF WHAT I THINK
"MY PEOPLE" SHOULD
BE, AND THEY DON'T
MEASURE UP. —SANDRA

TO BE HONEST, I'D RATHER JUST
MOVE ON AND FIND A NEW FRIEND
THAN STICK IT OUT. —CARRIE

I'M THE ONLY ONE
INVESTING IN THIS
FRIENDSHIP. —JENNIFER

FINDING AND KEEPING
AND GOING DEEP WITH
FRIENDS IS CHALLENGING
BECAUSE OF THE UNREALISTIC
EXPECTATIONS I HAVE OF
OTHERS. —GAYLA

STAYING FRIENDS AFTER
AN ARGUMENT IS JUST
TOO AWKWARD. I DON'T
KNOW HOW TO MOVE
PAST IT. —ELLA

9.

COMMITTED

■

| | TABLE | Goal: Consistency
Barrier: Conflict |

*I*F YOU'RE ACTIVELY PUTTING INTO ACTION ALL THE RELATIONAL principles and practices we've been exploring, you are for sure going to come to a moment in the very near future when you'll want to bail out on someone. Mark my words.

I was in the middle of writing this book when my sister-in-law Ashley called. "Can I come pick you up so we can go somewhere and talk?" she asked.

I assumed something difficult was happening in her life and, of course, said yes.

Ashley picked me up, and we drove to a park on a brilliant sunny day. As we sat in the car, she told me how I had said a few things recently that hurt her. She cried as she talked about how hard it was to bring this to me but how the candor was necessary. She didn't want to slowly start pulling back from me. She didn't want to "quit me," she said.

Those two words brought waves of fear crashing over my head. My immediate reaction was panic; was I about to lose another friend? And one who was a family member?

Shame came in and stayed.

What have I done? I keep hurting people!

Apparently I hurt people without even realizing it, and most often it is the people closest to me, whom I love most. I was already neck deep in writing this book, and had I learned nothing? Here I was, telling you to find your people, even as I was losing mine?

I breathed in and out. I listened. I waited.

Ashley and I both faced a choice as we sat in the car on that beautiful day. We could . . .

Self-protect.
Blame.
Pull back.
Even walk away.

Or we could fight.

Fight it out, fight for each other, fight to understand, and fight to stay.

After she laid out all the hurt she was feeling and why, Ashley said, "I am staying. This is me fighting for us."

In the days that followed that conversation, this thought frequently passed through me: *You aren't safe to be yourself with Ashley anymore, Jennie. You'll need to walk on eggshells from now on.*

Why was that my internal reaction? In bringing this hurt and conflict to me, Ashley was proving her safety. She was proving her love. She was proving her commitment to me.

She was not angry; she was hurt, and she wanted restoration. She didn't want me to pull back or to walk on eggshells.

Conflict should *make* friendships, not *break* them. If we don't run.

A few days later, when my fears had passed, Ashley and I went to dinner. I looked at her and said, "I love you so much. Telling me what you told me was such a gift to me. I am sorry. I was wrong. I am so sorry I hurt you. I never want to hurt you, but I did, and I will again. But still, I want you to feel safe with me. Tell me how to do that better, please."

The next thing she said was pure magic. Ashley gave me two super-easy, simple ways that I could love her well, things that were specific to her needs and our relationship. And in that moment, I realized I didn't need to quit, I didn't need to spiral in fear, and I didn't need to self-protect.

What I needed was to grow.

Conflict Is Part of Healthy Relationships

Conflict isn't the enemy to our friendships; conflict is fodder to make them grow. Conflict is inevitable in the kind of deep community we are talking about here. But handled biblically, it can strengthen and deepen our relationships.

I've made no secret that I view this book at least partly as an experiment in which you play an active role. I dream of you and others taking these practices from millennia of village life and applying them in your apartment complexes, in your suburban neighborhoods, in your dorms or urban townhomes.

I picture you opening doors to new friends, gathering by fires, asking better questions, sharpening others and being sharpened by them, and picking up a mission with a few people you love. I even picture you fighting! Yep. **Because I've never had a truly intimate friendship that was free of conflict.**

So I picture you fighting, stepping away for a moment— and I picture you coming back to the table, back to each other.

I believe that God is asking you and me to let people into our daily lives, into our deepest struggles, into our sin, into our routines, into our work, and into our dreams.

"Encourage one another and build each other up."
   "Bear one another's burdens."
   "Comfort one another."
   "Exhort one another every day."
   "Confess your sins to one another."
   "Forgive one another."[1]

The Bible is filled with such instructions for how we are to interact with others. If God is commanding us to forgive each other, then that means you and I are living in close enough proximity that I can reach you—and also hurt you. When He says that we are to bear one another's burdens, this means that I am close enough to get up under that burden alongside you and relieve some of the load. How can I confess my sin to or admonish you unless I can look you in the eye and tell you? You and I have to be *close* if we're going to keep these "one another" commandments.

We must become people who come close.

We must become people who engage.

We must become people who choose to stay.

Conflict in the Right Context

My biggest issue with community is that I too often hurt people or that they hurt me. It is a regular storyline. I mean, almost weekly some conflict has to be resolved in my life. That's just part of healthy community. **The hurt is part of the health**—it's weird to think about, but it's true.

I was recently talking with my brother-in-law Tony, who runs the dude ranch with my sister. As I explained the premise of this book, how we have to get back to living life in villages like every other generation, he shook his head and smirked as if to say, "I live in one of those, and it can be a mess!"

The actual words that came out of his mouth were, "Jennie, village life sounds great until you realize you're surrounded by a bunch of cannibals."

But what is true of the ranch is that it has a reputation for building leaders. It hires on boys and girls and eventually releases them into the world as leaders who are humble, as men and women with college degrees who have cleaned toilets, as healthy people who know how to work hard and love harder. Because sixty-plus people stuck in the middle of nowhere may look like a big mess, but all the messy sharpening is building character.

This happens because Brooke and Tony have laid down

some relational rules for their ranch staff. Things like, you have to say what you mean and mean what you say. And you keep short accounts with people instead of letting irritations fester into all-out war. And you speak highly of each other instead of gossiping or spreading half-truths. "Whenever a new set of staff members rolls in," Brooke once told me, "we get them addressing and resolving conflict within the first week, no exceptions. We live too close to each other and so we have to have a lot of hard conversations."

I laughed at Tony's cannibal comment, but Tony wasn't trying to be funny; he was being totally sincere, and I get it. The interactions at the ranch bear witness to a fundamental truth about human nature: the closer we are to other people, the more our rough edges will scrape them. Tony knows the cost of living with transparency and accountability. Tony knows the hurt he's felt and the hurt people he's shepherded in his little village. But that little village is changing lives not in spite of the conflict and hurts but because of the conflict and hurts.

But knowing the fruit that comes from healthy conflict doesn't take away its pain.

For too many of us, the pain we've suffered on previous occasions when we opened ourselves up to authentic community is so raw, so deep, so real, that we're reluctant to try again.

That's why we need relationships with God at the center and united in a shared mission. Without people pleasing, pride, and personal happiness at the center of our relationships, we live free enough to fight and humble enough to apologize and safe enough to work it out. People can disappoint you, and you can hurt other people, and forgiveness can be issued when we're looking to God, not others, for our hope, our identity, our purpose.

Because of Jesus, it really is possible to live this way.

Picture the scene on the night of the Last Supper. Jesus knew that the events leading to His crucifixion had been set in motion. He soon would be betrayed and hurt by nearly every one of His closest people. But in the midst of the hurt and rejection He must have been experiencing while sitting at the table with them, He pulled out bread and He broke it for His friends to eat. He poured wine for His friends to drink.

"Now as they were eating, Jesus took bread, and after blessing it broke it and gave it to the disciples, and said, 'Take, eat; this is my body.' And he took a cup, and when he had given thanks he gave it to them, saying, 'Drink of it, all of you, for this is my blood of the covenant, which is poured out for many for the forgiveness of sins.'"[2]

The ultimate table of reconciliation has been set, built on the broken body and spilled blood of our Savior.

This is why we can forgive.

It's why we can come together at the table with other sinners. We can, because He did. We can, because He made a way for us to be right with Him and right with each other.

Come to the Table

Throughout history and cultures, coming to a table, breaking bread together, has always represented reconciliation and healing.

In all my travels and conversations about the topic of community, this has come up again and again. From Italy to Africa, food. Meals. Tables. **People consistently and regularly come together around food.**

When we visited our family's small village in Italy, my uncle's cousin Luciano Fornaciari was waiting in the center of the little village of Sutri. He carried a huge American flag and bore a beautiful, wide smile. He hugged us tight, though we'd never met. We were family, and we were about to see what that meant in Italian villages.

Cousin Luciano hustled us through the quiet cobblestone streets into his sister's restaurant, which was packed with couples, friends, kids, and the elderly all eating lunch together. He led us into the back room to a table that seated at least twenty-five people, all of whom he was related to. Suddenly my family was bombarded with exuberant Italian greetings and joyously suffocating hugs. We may not have been related by blood, but we were their family.

We sat down to lunch with grandparents, in-laws, kids of all ages, and felt like royalty.

Six full courses.

Lots of laughter.

Lots of time.

Lots of people talking over each other.

Lots of love.

Lots of . . . fighting.

Did I mention the fighting?

I didn't understand the language, but we recognized anger and frustration. We knew what was meant by the shaking of fists.

My uncle's cousin was the only English speaker, and he told me a little of what was playing out. Then he said, "No worries. This is how it goes."

For generations the members of this family had all lived within blocks of each other in the same tiny village where they were born. They'll likely be back at that same table for lunch tomorrow.

Conflict is safe when you know you won't quit each other.

But we must agree not to quit.

Now, hear me. Sometimes the relationship might need to end. Maybe it is just so toxic that you need to separate or set more stringent boundaries. Or you have tried to reconcile and come to understanding multiple times, but the friendship continues in disagreement and dissension. You've done a lot of work to resolve it, but it's not happening.

The apostle Paul went through this with multiple relationships. Paul and Peter worked things out, but they stayed away from each other for the most part. Paul and Barnabas went separate ways, and it ended up serving the gospel.

But if you quit, that will mean you start over in finding your people. Guess what? The new people are going to hurt you too. Or you will hurt them. Or both. Because we all do.

If you stay, you work through it and grow stronger together.

How many times have you avoided or even ghosted someone who could have possibly been a forever friend if you did the work and didn't run?

Conflict is a part of life, and we have to figure out how to deal with it in a way that honors and glorifies God to the rest of the world.

How Do We Do This?

Let's get really practical. How can we have healthy conflict?

1. Assume the Best

If we're going to deal with an offense, it needs to be a real offense. This is my rule on when to address something: don't react too quickly. So many hurts are just misunderstandings. We can make up this whole narrative in our heads about what someone thinks from one thing they said or did. The other person doesn't even know anything's amiss, while we're in all-out-war mode! Instead, assume the best and try to move on. We can do this because our hope is heaven, where our citizenship truly is. **We are satisfied in our relationship with God so we can be content with people being people.** We can let them disappoint us and just let it go.

2. Keep Short Accounts

If you can't let that thing go, then go to that person. Ask them what they meant by that. You might have misunderstood them, so give them space to explain. But no matter what, don't let bitterness fester. Paul said, "In your anger do not sin. Do not let the sun go down while you are still angry."[3] In other words, don't keep a running tab of the other person's faults or sins.

3. Be Quick to Apologize

When someone says you've caused them pain or harm, be quick to apologize and ask what you can do to make amends. You don't need to say much else. In fact, the more you say, the more it turns into defending yourself.

I've learned that there is very little good done in defending myself, even if my actions or intentions were right. I can't tell you how many times people have brought me something that hurt them, and I didn't even know I'd sinned. There was no ill intention, no purposeful hurt, and I didn't even realize I had said or done the things that so clearly caused pain. That doesn't matter. They felt hurt, specifically by me. **I take responsibility for hurting them, even if I didn't mean to.**

King David never defended his own name. He held people back from defending his name. He was comfortable with being misunderstood or people thinking ill of him. He knew God would defend what deserved to be defended. God is the defender of our names, which means we get to live unoffendable.

4. Aim to Be a Peacemaker

If you think someone is upset with you, but they haven't come to you with a concern, what can you do?

I'm a big believer in getting everything out on the table. Don't spend time trying to construct a story around what someone might be thinking about you. Instead, just pick up the phone and call or send a text and make sure the two of you are okay.

In doing this, sometimes I learn that everything's great,

sometimes I'm able to resolve a problem before it blows up between us, and sometimes the person says that nothing is wrong but I can clearly see there's something building inside. Here's the verse I live by: "If it is possible, as far as it depends on you, live at peace with everyone."[4] I will do what I can, but I can't control that other person or make them tell me if something is upsetting them. I can't force it to be okay. I can rest knowing I've done everything I can.

Choosing Inconvenience

But the challenge before us is deeper than just conflict resolution. It's choosing to prioritize each other again and again, committing consistent time day in and day out. Sometimes that means we get hurt, and sometimes it means we are simply inconvenienced.

Throughout history most people stuck together because they were literally stuck together—for the entirety of their lives, no less. You live in an Italian village of fifty people and get in a fight? Tough. You are at the only little Italian grocer (owned by the person you are fighting with) the next day, picking up carrots, pasta, and biscuit cookie thingies.

But these days too many of us are experts at quitting each other, and most of us can figure out a way to hide from everyone while we do it.

What I am calling you to instead, what Paul was calling us to, what God is calling us to, is a wholly different, supernatural mindset that is guarded, supplied, and filled with Christ Jesus. He is the way we think, relate, speak, reconcile, forgive, and love. Because we've been given such abundance, we give away our abundance. This is our story. This is how we live out the gospel.

We choose to be inconvenienced for the sake of each other.

If you think about it, friendship—all relationships, really—is a giant inconvenience, at least if we're doing it right. **And the inconvenience chosen again and again changes us, wakes us up, makes us laugh and love and hope and dream.**

Yeah, intertwining my life with other people is inconvenient, but I'll take that kind of trouble again and again over the ease and emptiness of trying to go it alone.

To leave behind our loneliness and enjoy the reward of community we have to keep showing up, keep being vulnerable, keep coming to the table. Be together, work together, and share life together—over and over again. Then one day we look up and realize our friendships have grown deep.

The Science of Clocking Time with People

One reason it's so hard to have good friends is that getting something on the calendar takes so much work. So first put something regular on your calendar. It takes the work out of this. Schedule it like I did with my friends in Austin. Pick the time and place where you'll all show up.

Second, once you have found your close people, break all the rules of how you spend time together:

- Purposefully leave your house a mess.
- Invite someone to your dinner party an hour early to help with prep or ask them to stay late and help you clean up.

- Leave your laundry out on the couch and ask them to help you fold.
- Ask if they'll pick your kid up on their way over.
- Borrow the ingredient you forgot instead of running to the store to buy it.
- Bother someone to run the errand with you.
- Stop by someone's house unannounced.
- Bring someone a meal without warning.
- Ask to borrow clothes for a special event instead of shopping for a new dress.
- Ask someone to help you clean out your closet.
- Offer to help someone paint a room.
- Ask to join someone else's family dinner.

(That last one's truly bold.)

The suggestions above may be way outside your comfort zone, but I am here to tell you that unless and until you and I get serious about logging time with people—significant, consistent time—we simply can't enjoy the level of friendship we long for, the kind of relationship that makes us feel connected and known. How do I know this? Because a few very smart people have quantified what it takes to be a friend.

I mentioned earlier that it takes two hundred hours together for an acquaintance to become a close friend. Let me tell you where that little tidbit came from. The University of Oxford evolutionary psychologist Robin Dunbar said our relational spheres comprise layers of people who fall into categories such as acquaintances, casual friends, friends, good friends, and intimate friends. But what was groundbreaking about his work was the fact that he put numbers to those categories. While we can maintain roughly 150 meaningful relationships at a time, he suggested only fifty of those people would be considered "friends" and only five would be considered "intimate friends."

Inspired by Dunbar's research, University of Kansas professor Jeffrey Hall began poking around at those various relational layers: How did a meaningful relationship move from being a casual friend, say, to a friend? What type of investment was needed for this transition to occur? How long would it take? The results of the research he dove into are fascinating to me. As reported in *Psychology Today*, "He found that it took about 50 hours of interaction to move from acquaintance to casual friend, about 90 hours to move from casual friend to friend, and more than 200 hours to qualify as a best friend."[5]

This all begs the question: **With the people you consider your most intimate friends, how many hours have you logged?** That impromptu trip to the mall that lasted a couple of hours? That's 1 percent of an intimate relationship logged. The cookout in your backyard that spans an entire summer's afternoon? You've just racked up 3 percent of a ride-or-die friendship. The constant togetherness at the two-day women's retreat? That's a good 25 percent right there. My guess is that the reason you feel close to certain people is that you have faithfully put in the time together.

Any guesses as to where to find that kind of time when we're all too busy for friends? Yep. Mealtime—while you're prepping, cooking, eating, and cleaning up food.

My team, my small group, Zac's family, my kids and all their friends—if I cook, someone will usually show up. My kids have learned to ask, "Is there enough for [fill in a number] people?" And sometimes there isn't, but lots of times, it just works.

We have to become people who stay. We have to become friends who show up to chop things for a few hours and stay even later to do the dishes, not just to eat. And we need to do this consistently, time and time again.

I'm convinced a key reason for our loneliness is that we give up too easily. Friendships take time—a *lot* of time. A lot of working it out. A lot of showing up. A lot of cleaning out closets. A lot of tears. A lot of laughter. A lot of food. A lot of inconvenience.

We give up so easily because it's costly. It's messy. It's hard.

It *is* hard. Take a minute. Breathe in and accept that truth. Okay.

Now hear me: you can do hard things.

God is with you, in you, and for you. You, my friend, can show up.

You can hurt someone and apologize. You can be hurt and forgive.

You can choose consistency and inconvenience.

And the friendship you gain will be worth it.

YOUR TURN

LOGGING CONSISTENT TIME TOGETHER

—

COMMIT TO A DAY AND A TIME TO INVEST CONSISTENTLY with a small group of friends every week for the next six months. Here's how:

1. Pick your people.

   ——

2. Invite them to gather more regularly.

   ——

3. Pick your time and location and keep it consistent.

   ——

4. Decide how long you're going to commit to this. It's okay to set an end date.

   ——

5. Discuss together how you plan to handle conflict.

Ideas for Embracing
the Inconvenience of Friendship

· · · · · ·

- Who in your friend group needs to be supported? Organize a way for everyone to do something nice for that person.
- Reach out to a friend who is pulling away from you and/or God, someone who is isolating herself. Take over a meal and check on her.
- Ask your friend to pray together with you.
- Let go of minor offenses and truly move on.
- Don't gossip when you have been wronged.
- Pray about a hurt you experience before talking through it with your friend.
- Be the one who says, "I feel like things aren't right between us. Is there anything we should talk through?"
- After you have reconciled, or if you've chosen to simply let go of a hurt, treat your friend normally the next time you see her.
- Send a casual, lighthearted text about something you can do together.

BUT WHAT ABOUT . . .

> *. . . if my spouse complains about how much*
> *time I'm spending with other people?*

This is a tough one. Because community could be a bigger priority for you than for your spouse, it's important you have a unified perspective on how to incorporate it into your lives. You both need this. My suggestion: read this book together and build a shared vision for how to pursue deeper relationships.

> *. . . if I hardly ever have conflict in friendship?*
> *Is that a bad sign?*

Not necessarily. You might be a laid-back person who isn't easily offended. But be sure you are not secretly holding on to any bitterness if you have a less combative personality. And be sure you aren't playing it too safe with your current friendships or caught up in people pleasing. Are you saying the hard things? Are you being honest with your feelings?

> *. . . how to determine how much hanging out*
> *is too much? I know I shouldn't live in a*
> *bubble with my favorite people.*

This is why I love the pattern of mission built into our friendships. Hopefully we're noticing the people around us who need God or need deeper friendships and we're constantly

pulling them in. Hopefully we are, out of our healthy friendships, ministering and loving people intentionally. If mission
is a part of your close friendships, they won't become stagnant.
But friendships always get unhealthy if they aren't focused on
a life-giving purpose.

PART

3

. . .

FIGHTING FOR YOUR VILLAGE

. . .

10.

FINDING YOUR FAMILY

■

*L*AST WEEK A HANDFUL OF FRIENDS CAME OVER, MOSTLY SINGLE friends from work and some young marrieds with babies. The subject of family came up, and each person told stories not of their nuclear families but of families they frequently visit for dinner or have lived with at various points in their lives.

Logan talked about living with the McFarlins before she and her husband had the income to find their own place. Hannah talked about all the singles who lived with her parents while she was growing up and how she missed those big, extended-family dinners. Another friend mentioned her grandfather, who had lived with her family when she and her siblings were young.

Caroline, our sitter turned IFtern turned friend, laughed and, looking at me, said, "I'm basically your adopted daughter, based on how much time I've spent with you and your family."

The Shifting Definition of Family

It's possible that you are still looking around and wondering who your village is. But I hope you are learning to see that the potential for a diverse huddle of humans to love and to love you back is everywhere!

Family is God's very first, best place for us to learn and live community. But what we think of as family is a far cry from His original design. You can try, but no amount of research is going to turn up ancient evidence of a mom, a dad, and 2.5 kids living on their own, fenced off from everyone else, on a one-third-acre plot of land. What you will find, if you go hunting for details on how things used to be, is a whole lot of communal living.

Ages ago, when the average life span saw people dying far younger than they do today, the concept of family included everyone from parents and grandparents and aunts and uncles to half siblings, neighbors, cousins, coworkers, and friends who felt like family but actually weren't. The idea of a single-family dwelling hadn't yet been invented, which meant that to be human was to be surrounded by other humans—in villages, nearly 100 percent of the time.

Everything shifted in the 1920s after a social anthropologist named Bronislaw Malinowski coined the term "nuclear family" in reference to a social unit consisting solely of 2 parents and their 2.5 children. The concept of the nuclear family revolutionized marketing because a small, insulated, defined group of people made excellent consumer targets for everything from diapers to Crock-Pots.

The fewer things people shared, the more they individually had to buy.

It worked. Toaster sales went through the roof.

Meanwhile, our understanding of family shrank, singles were isolated, young mamas were left feeling alone to raise their kids, and elderly people were marginalized. We hid behind taller fences, alone, with our shiny new toasters.

Or at least, most of us did. Some of us, thankfully, still recognize the beauty built into God's original plan.

During the pandemic, my friend Tasha let me know that her great-aunt had contracted COVID-19. "She's seventy-seven years old," Tasha said, "and she has a caretaker who comes in a couple of times a week to help her. Evidently one of her caretakers was sick when she came to help her last week, and now she's sick."

Tasha's great-aunt lives in North Carolina. After sharing a home for years with her own mother, she was now trying to live on her own. But because the great-aunt had a positive COVID-19 test, caretakers weren't allowed entry into her house, and Tasha was worried.

"Her sister is going to come down from New York and stay with her for at least a month," Tasha then said, "so that ought to help."

"Your great-aunt's sister, who is probably also in her seventies or even her eighties, is going to leave her home in New York to go live in North Carolina for an entire month?" I asked.

"Yeah, of course," Tasha said.

She went on to tell me that in most Black communities

"we take care of our family members, and our neighbors become like family." She said, "We are in it together, Jennie— life, loss, victory, sorrow, COVID-19, the whole bit. We are *in it*, no matter what."

In addition to this sister relocating for weeks on end to care for a loved one, Tasha told me that family members who were local had already arranged a meal train to ensure that the woman didn't miss a single meal. Tasha herself had hit up Amazon to deliver every nonperishable she could think of to her ailing great-aunt.

All this struck me as quite a sacrifice and honestly also quite beautiful, and I said so. Then Tasha reminded me that collective living is just "how things are" in communities like hers. "African Americans live intergenerationally," she said, "and will do whatever it takes to take care of each other."

Taking care of one another.

Isn't that what we all crave?

And yet something in us resists the thought of relying on others and of others relying on us.

When a friend of mine got married a few years ago, his new wife, a white American, initially appreciated the underpinnings of his Asian culture—the way families stuck together, the way grown kids cared for their aging elders, and so forth. Then he floated the idea of his mother, a widow, coming to live with them and . . . let's just say it felt harder to appreciate the culture that looked so rich in theory.

Many of us are failing miserably when it comes to taking care of one another, and while this isn't a book about caring for aging parents, it was one of the most convicting things I observed about different people both within our culture and around the world. They take care of their families. In fact, they stick together all their lives.

The Original Family Plan

I told you earlier that I believe with all my heart that the first, best community God created was the family. During creation, on day six He built His masterpiece: humans. Adam. Eve. A man and his wife, who could then procreate and have children. A family—made in the image of God.

Right from the start God determined that it was never good for a person to be alone, to live alone, to exist separate from other persons, and so God put forth His solution: ready-made community, for you and for me. From that moment onward, whenever life felt hard or scary or frustrating, we'd have people to come home to, someone to lean on, shoulders on which to bury our tearstained faces. A friend. Our family would be there for us, and we would be there for them. This would not be a come-and-go arrangement but rather a covenant commitment.

We would stick together through every season, seeing, knowing, loving, serving.

We would practice relating within the four walls of our home so that when we went out into the world, we would know how to love others well.

We would know how to ask good questions because we practiced good question-asking at home.

We would know how to show empathy to hurting people because we practiced empathetic communication at home.

We would know how to live unoffended because we practiced letting go of our hurts at home.

We would know how to extend earnest forgiveness because we practiced forgiving others at home.

We would know how to work through differences and disagreements because we practiced effective conflict resolution at home.

Family was supposed to be our first community, a gathering of people who accepted and loved us and then taught us to accept and love others well. **This was God's original plan, both to bless people within families and then to bless *through families* the rest of the world.** "God places the lonely in families," the psalmist promised; "he sets the prisoners free and gives them joy."[1]

I've always loved that verse because of the comparison between family members and prisoners who have been freed. The picture of the family ought to be a picture of outright freedom, of chains being thrown off, of joy. Which is why historically it was not considered a big deal to set aside our own desires and care for those in our family. I'm thinking here of exhortations such as the one in 1 Timothy, where the apostle Paul reminded his young protégé that family matters: "Those who won't care for their relatives, especially those in their own household, have denied the true faith. Such people are worse than unbelievers."[2]

Pretty harsh language, right? So harsh that it nearly reads as hyperbole, as in, "*Of course* we care for the members of our family, Timothy. I mean, this is so obvious that I probably don't even need to say it."

The "relatives" part to those living in Paul's day would include not only those in your immediate family, but also extended family members and even the stranger who was passing by and needed a place to stay, food to eat, or short-term care of some other kind. Some historians suggest that this gathering of related people could have numbered up to one hundred, a far cry from the 2.63 people in the modern family of today.[3] Your *household* included all those you were responsible for. Those you willingly cared for. Those with whom you'd rise or fall.

You'd share meals with these people.

You'd do chores with these people.

You'd raise children with these people.

You'd labor with these people.

You'd entertain dreams with these people.

You'd swap stories with these people.

You'd work through disagreements with these people.

You'd celebrate wins with these people.

You'd grieve disappointments with these people.

You'd welcome new babies with these people.

You'd bury loved ones with these people.

You'd do all the stuff of life with these people. And you'd do this every day.

But Let's Be Real. Family Is Hard.

All this togetherness built into God's plan for family probably begs a question: *What if these people we call family consistently drive us absolutely crazy?!* Or far worse, they are completely absent or abusive?

I know. I hear your stories of unthinkable atrocities committed by family members. First, hear me clearly: toxic abuse absolutely requires boundaries and perhaps estrangement. Please seek help if you are in that position now or if you experienced it growing up and have never healed from it. No one should go through that alone.

But for most of us, our family members aren't truly toxic. They just drive us crazy! Or maybe we just don't like some of them.

Maybe they are critical of how you parent or what you want to do after college.

Maybe they pressure you to get married or to vote the same way they do.

Maybe they manipulate you with money or correct your grammar or complain constantly that you never come to visit.

Or maybe, like my friend's brother, they come and stay for too long and expect you to take care of them at Christmas.

If we have our preference, we usually seek out intimate relationships with people who don't drive us too crazy, aren't critical, and are a lot like us. **But with family you don't get to pick your people. Which means that most likely they won't all be easy to love.**

When we were adopting Cooper, we read a lot about family attachment and how disruptive it can be to a soul to lose the first relationships that were supposed to be everything. It still makes me cry as I type this because while adoption is redemptive, it fundamentally arises from the most unimaginable disruption: the loss of the people who brought you into existence.

When attachment with your first relationships breaks down in any way and for any reason, attachment becomes difficult and scary on any level. It's why if you sign up for therapy tomorrow, in the first twenty minutes you'll be asked about your relationship with your parents.

The good news is that we can learn a better way to relate, and we absolutely can heal. I've experienced it.

I was thirty years old when I sat down with my dad to tell him how I lived with a limp from the hurts he had inadvertently brought into my life. At the time I was a young parent myself but still didn't realize how easy it is to wound your kids.

I wrote my dad a six-page letter, three pages of gratitude and three pages of wounds, and read it aloud. It felt important. I had done the work, including years of counseling, but I had never shared with him the hurt that some of his behaviors had caused me.

This was the day, and yet I couldn't conceive of any good that would come from this conversation I knew I needed to have. First, I didn't want to hurt my dad. Second, I couldn't see how this would end well. Either my dad would criticize me, validating my worst fears, or he would shrug it off and casually say that he hadn't meant anything by his words and actions. In short, invalidating the hurts of my childhood.

Here's the beautiful truth about my earthly daddy: he loves Jesus, he loves his family, and he has spent his entire life trying to be a good father and a loving husband. As his daughter, I have so much to be thankful for. And yet I still walked away from my upbringing with baggage, hurt, and a bit of a spiraling identity crisis. **We all carry attachment issues into adulthood because we all have sinners for parents.**

My dad listened to every word I said that day. He cried happy tears over my gratitude for tuck-ins and for his working tirelessly to provide for us. He cried bitter ones when I carefully explained how I'd often feared that I was never enough in his estimation.

He cried. He listened. And then he did something I couldn't have imagined prior to this conversation: he told me about his relationship with his mom and his dad. In short, he said, "Jennie, I messed up. It was my fault, not yours. And let me tell you where I first heard the message that I had to be perfect: it was from my mom and dad. I heard that message, I absorbed that message, and then I passed that message on to you."

We love others in the manner in which we ourselves were loved. Equally true: we tend to hurt others in the manner in which we ourselves have been hurt. The cycle perpetuates itself until something interrupts it and someone says, "Enough."

That's what Dad and I did that day. In unison, we said, "Enough."

Finding Your Family

Of course, not every family relationship can be successfully healed and restored. So, if you have a broken relationship with your parents or other family members, is it hopeless?

In anthropology, there is a term that strikes at the core of what I see happening in the lives of people all over the world who long for a healthy family, even as their relatives seem to spiral out of control. The term *fictive kinship*—which I think is a fancy term for "find your people"—refers to strong social ties that aren't established by marriage or by blood.[4] Interestingly, some researchers assert that the happiest people are those who have the strongest fictive-kinship bonds: their own family was a disaster, so they went and formed a new one to call their own.

In Okinawa, this is carried out in social support groups called *moais*—literally, "meeting for a common purpose."[5] When kids are born on this island, they are connected with up to five other children, a pod of people they will be committed to for the entirety of their lives. It is quite literally their second family, even if their first family is life giving and kind. They play with that group. Later, they will work with that group. Still later, they will raise children, tend to each other when one falls ill, loan each other money when one falls on tough times, and grow old, all within the context of that group.

In central Mexico, parents from different families band together to raise their children in a form of fictive kinship called *compadrazgo*—literally, "coparenting."[6]

In Rwanda, as I said before, older men parent younger males as though those boys were their own.

We could examine myriad cultures, but the point would be the same: in nearly every culture, we see this phenomenon of coming together to plug the holes that natural families will not or cannot fill.

When I asked Pastor Charles about the generation of boys and girls who grew up in Rwanda after being left fatherless by the horrific genocide there in the mid-1990s, he said, "Jennie, the solution to that fatherlessness is the Church. We can't bring back their earthly fathers, so we give those children spiritual fathers instead."

A Family Is Waiting for You

One of my favorite things about God is that He can meet our needs as a loving, caring, intimate parent in a way no earthly parent can. Whether you feel like an orphan and are craving to be "set in a family" or you have a healthy family but you still feel lonely, God has built a beautiful family for you to be part of—His own. In fact, at the very core of the gospel message is this idea that, despite our being separated from God because of our sin, in His great love God has a plan to get us back.

He invites us into His family. He adopts us in from the moment we trust Jesus as Savior. And He gives us a place with brothers and sisters and promises to be a loving Father for us and to help us in our distress. He is our family, and through His Church, we have a new, bigger family here on earth.

"You have received the Spirit of adoption as sons, by whom we cry, 'Abba! Father!'" Scripture reminds us. "For we are the temple of the living God. As God has said: 'I will live with them and walk among them, and I will be their God, and they will be my people.'"[7]

One of the greatest village experiences Zac and I have known involved a fumbling, imperfect church plant set in the context of a diverse crew of really kind sinners. These days, our small group through our church has become like family. I have brothers, sisters, grandparents, cousins, and crazy aunts galore, and it all has come through our local, real-life church.

But for you, "church" may usher in a completely different set of thoughts.

For most people I talk to, the only collection of individuals that comes remotely close to having caused as much pain and trauma as their nuclear family is the local church. Any guesses why? Because it's full of sinners. And guess what sinners do?

Yep. They sin.

We hurt each other. One of the reasons people leave the church is because it doesn't feel like a family. It's not a group of people coming together to take care of each other under the banner of Jesus. No, these days, you're lucky if you know a single soul at your church. We're more often a bunch of strangers who silently pass each other by.

But it doesn't have to be this way. As followers of Jesus, we need each other, and as difficult as it might feel, a local church is one of the best ways to find your people.

I tell my teammates when they come to work at IF:Gathering, "Find an imperfect church fast, and start serving in the nursery." By serving right away, you will meet people, and even though those people won't be perfect, those connections with real, living beings will help you remember that you are part of something good. And serving also reminds you, before you resent the Church too much, that you are part of it. You are the Church. It isn't an institution, it's a group of people, of which you are one.

Church can be our people.

Church can be our imperfect little village.

Church can be our family.

The Art of Staying

If I could say just one thing to you and to everyone who has started believing that they are destined for loneliness, it's this: **What if you are missing potentially beautiful, life-giving** friendships that are waiting for you right inside your family or right down the street at a local church?

Scripture is full of flourishing fictive-kinship relationships that ought to inform how we interact today. In other words, there are probably some stand-in family members all around you, ready to accept and encourage and love you, if only you'd choose to see them that way, if you would let them in, if you would commit to them.

Yes. It's difficult and costly. I am a family member and I am a church member, and I know what a mess I can be and I know what a mess you can be too. But here's what else I know: there is nothing quite like having a full table of broken people who, like my Italian family, fight and laugh and celebrate and talk over each other and show up and love and criticize and toast.

"Those who love their dream of a Christian community more than the Christian community itself become destroyers of that Christian community," Dietrich Bonhoeffer wrote.[8]

As a starting point to committing to our family, whether by blood, adoption, or choice: let's be careful about how we talk about our family.

"My church keeps asking for money."

"My father has always been a jerk."

"My family has never understood me."

"Why isn't my church caring for _____?"

"They will never accept me."

"We've all agreed to just part ways."

"It will never work for us to be in each other's lives."

"We just can't get along."

"My family is a dysfunctional mess."

"It's irreparable, my relationship with my mom."

"I'm better off without them."

Whenever we make statements like this, we give ourselves permission to start a construction project that erects sky-high walls. We then spend the rest of our lives making sure we stay on our side of the wall and that "they" remain on theirs. Out of sight, out of mind is the approach we take, almost forgetting those people exist until the bothersome thought creeps in from time to time: *I wonder what might have been.*

Instead of committing ourselves to isolation, let's consider a better commitment. It's what the Benedictine monks call the vow of stability. "By making a vow of stability," Trappist monk Thomas Merton once wrote,

> The monk renounces the vain hope of wandering off to a find a "perfect monastery." This implies a deep act of faith: the recognition that it does not much matter where we are or whom we live with. . . . Stability becomes difficult for a man whose monastic idea contains some note, some element of the extraordinary. All monasteries are more or less ordinary. . . . Its ordinariness is one of its greatest blessings.[9]

After all the other vows are made and upheld by a monk, the vow of stability is his way of saying to the other brothers, "Despite the nuances and failures and ordinariness of you people, I'm in this for the long haul. I'm a stayer. I'm part of you, and you're part of me. I'm here. I'll be here. I'll never go anywhere." I can't think of a better way to describe what it means to be a family.

Engraved on my husband's wedding ring, as on many rings in the world, is a reference to Ruth 1:16–17, which says, "Where you go I will go, and where you lodge I will lodge. Your people shall be my people, and your God my God. Where you die I will die, and there will I be buried."

Ruth was Naomi's daughter-in-law. After her husband, Naomi's son, died, she made this commitment to her mother-in-law. Her mother-in-law! She could have gone back to her family of origin, but she committed in love to stay and live and even die with this woman. **She chose to stay, to consider this woman her family.**

My husband at times has felt like my best friend in my village and at times my greatest enemy. But we have fought for each other and our relationship, because we are committed to stay. We choose to stay. In imperfect marriages, in imperfect churches, in imperfect friendships.

What will you choose?

What Changes When You Choose to Stay?

Choosing to stay is not easy, but whomever God has given you as your family . . .

the moment you decide to accept them for who they are instead of constantly trying to get them to change . . .

the moment you look for ways to serve your family and church instead of constantly expecting things from them . . .

the moment you watch for opportunities to speak an encouraging word instead of questioning their every decision . . .

the moment you seek out chances to love them well instead of spending your days anticipating awful exchanges with them . . .

that might be the moment when you see your family and church changed.

Perhaps you've heard of confirmation bias, which is when you find in the world exactly what you expect to find. Confirmation bias works here too. If you expect to find beauty in your family relationships, you will find beauty. If you expect to find support, then you will find support. If you expect to find acceptance, then you will find acceptance.

If you expect to find friendship, then nine times out of ten, guess what?

You will find a friend.

My daddy today is the least critical person in my life. He in fact has transformed into my greatest cheerleader. He goes out of his way constantly to tell me how proud he is of me, how much I mean to him. And that never gets old. I see the beauty in our relationship now; in fact, it's all I see.

It's all I want to see.

Don't miss the imperfect people right in front of you.

11.

HOLDING ON TO
YOUR PEOPLE

■

I WANT TO GIVE YOU A BIGGER, MORE BEAUTIFUL VISION FOR living neck deep in interconnected, diverse community. I want you to walk away from this book committed to prioritizing that community over better job offers, more square footage, or a cooler city. I want you to see God's vision for healthy relationships and to choose that above comfort or easy, shallow conversations or occasional convenient meetups. I want you to not only find your inner circle but to find a village where you can know and serve and be served and known. I want you to find your people.

But the vision is so much bigger than that.

It's for you to embrace a completely different way to live.

Because I see it in Scripture, and I know it's possible. Even so, it will always be hard.

An Enemy Is Wrestling Against Us

Scripture says, "We do not wrestle against flesh and blood, but against the rulers, against the authorities, against the cosmic powers over this present darkness, against the spiritual forces of evil in the heavenly places."[1] This is the battle we're in. We must remember this.

Years ago, in the early days of our church plant, I was in a big disagreement with someone in the church. I felt misunderstood, and she felt misunderstood. So we sat down to talk about it. After trying to work it out, it blew up even more. I left our meeting even madder than I'd been before, not knowing how to resolve the thing.

I don't know if you've ever been in conflict like that, in which even though you're trying, even though you're sitting down and going through the steps of resolution, it feels like resolution just can't be found. When I read that verse above in Ephesians, I realized the problem wasn't Heather. The problem was the enemy who was trying to divide us.

As we discussed in chapter 4, the enemy hates community. His goal is to divide us, to distract us, to separate us so he can prevent us from being most effective. **If every believer on earth was united and of one mind on mission together, the Church would be unbelievably dangerous.** We would see revival in every city and every country. More kingdom work would be taking place than we could possibly imagine. So, of course, the most effective way for the enemy to stop the work of God on earth is to have us devour each other instead of celebrating each other and loving each other and serving each other and working together. This is why I care so much about developing deep, authentic, committed community.

Investing in relationship is not about pursuing our own happiness. It's not just so that we can have friends to go to dinner with when we feel lonely. It's so that we can be effective for eternity. It's so that people will come to know Christ because of our love. It's so that our love would speak so boldly and clearly of Jesus that it would be contagious, that it would cause other people to want to follow God.

The enemy's tactics to subvert God's good plan for our relationships are things you are very familiar with:

- codependency
- independence
- busyness
- gossip
- comparison
- laziness
- fear

I want to take a little time here to discuss each of these tactics, lest you do all this work to find your people only to not know how to hang on to them over the long haul.

The Trap of Codependency

You might be thinking, *What in the world does that psychobabble word even mean?*

The short answer: a codependent relationship is when one

person's happiness is dependent on the other to a dispropor-
tionate level. Codependency develops when we look to other
people to meet our needs instead of looking to God. It usually
begins as people pleasing—or the converse, expecting people
to meet all our needs. Either of these will grow into a whole
slew of unhealthy behaviors. **Relationships always go wrong
when God is not in the center.**

When you go into a relationship—whether with your
spouse or your roommate or your friend—looking for that person to meet a need, to solve a problem, to fulfill you in ways only
God can, that relationship will become destructive. Codependent relationships are built with a goal that can never be reached.
That human will disappoint you 100 percent of the time.

And that's okay. I've learned to see disappointments in relationships as reminders that God is enough for me.

How do you know if you are in a codependent relationship?

One sign is that you constantly feel discouraged and disappointed by the person. When you have an extreme reaction
to something, you need to pay attention because it's probably
evidence of something or someone you've made into an idol.
When you are unusually upset that a person didn't call or that
person wasn't loving enough toward you or didn't invite you to
something, ask yourself, *Am I putting unfair expectations on this
person to meet my needs?*

It is okay to have needs in a relationship and even expectations. We all have them. But are they fair expectations? Are
they clear expectations? Are you looking to someone to meet
needs that only God can meet?

The Trap of Independence

We know we need each other in a million different ways in life, but those of us who don't battle with codependency often fall into the trap of living independently. At our very core God built us to be fragile, finite, needy creatures so we would come to Him and so we would lean into the strengths and gifts of one another.

If there is one principle that has shaped my last three years of ministry, it is this: **pull people in at every turn.** Never do anything alone. Why? Because even God exists in community within Himself.

If you want to be effective, then ask for help. This makes other people feel needed, draws them together in a shared purpose. What's more, by taking this simple but vulnerable step, we start to build the community we are longing for.

Today I was preparing my notes for a talk I'm giving this weekend. I got the message to a place where I was satisfied, and then I was ready to move on to something else. Instead, I called Chloe, who runs beside me every day in this calling, and I said, "Please, help me with this talk."

As we've already established, I hate asking for help.

I don't want to bother my friend/teammate at the end of a long day.

Plus, I'm prideful. I felt confident that I had everything ready to go.

But because of my conviction that no one should do anything alone, I asked for help. Chloe's fresh eyes, her creativity, and her questions elevated a good talk into a great one. She helped me see what I'd missed and tighten things up.

Anything helpful I send out into the world has been shaped by at least a handful of other people, and I'm not ashamed of that fact.

It is God's plan to bring the best work out of community! Always has been and always will be.

Ask for help.

Build a team.

Collaborate.

Don't create or live isolated.

Every one of us needs people, so ask a friend for something and do not apologize when you do. It is a lie from the devil that we should be independent and self-sufficient!

The Trap of Busyness

Are you busy? Great. Bring people along. Invest in relationships as you are going.

I discipled a young woman eighteen years ago, back when she was a teenager and I was floundering through the baby years of parenting. Now she is neck deep in the stage of life of young kids. At dinner recently, Bethany named all the things that she remembers about my spending time with her:

1. You called me friend.
2. You zeroed in on me and really listened.
3. You squeezed me tight whenever you saw me.
4. You showed me grace.
5. You used to teach your toddlers about sin while you were driving and I sat in the front seat.

What influenced her most wasn't the brilliant Bible study I led—as much as I wish that had been true. It was all the small things, our mundane interactions as we were just living, that made her feel seen.

The takeaway here? Invite a teenager or young woman along on your carpool drives. Take her to coffee or for a walk. Lead that study in your house while kids nap or crawl all over you. Take a coworker to lunch. Invite the newlyweds over for dessert. Find the lonely college girl in your town. *Please. Today.*

This is how we change the world.

How many people has Bethany discipled since I discipled her? She couldn't count them all, because this has been the marker of her life. She reminded me that I made her lead a study for her peers at age sixteen! And she just never stopped after that. Bethany, Ali, Christi, Cassie, Courtney, Emily, Jen, Amanda, Pam, Katherine, and others are the best investments of my life. That's just a few I've poured into, and those few have discipled others, with exponential, immeasurable numbers of people they have discipled behind them.

The Trap of Gossip

Once I was venting to my sister about someone, and sure enough, I had pocket dialed one of the friends of the person I was complaining about and they listened to the whole thing. I'll never forget it! God had that happen because it was such a reminder that this is not okay, *ever.* Now when I am tempted to talk about other people behind their backs, I always picture them walking up behind us and how they might feel if they heard my words.

If you have friends who are constantly talking with you about other people, let me tell you a little secret: when you're not there, they're talking about you!

The truth is, if gossip didn't feel good, we wouldn't do it. Something in us—something unhealthy and twisted—likes having the inside track on some juicy tidbit or feeling a little superior as we engage in criticism of someone else.

But so often we end up so discouraged after our time with friends, having fixated on negative things rather than choosing to celebrate the good in others.

Romans 8:6 tells us that there's a road that leads to sin and death and a road that leads to life and peace. How do we stay on the road to life and peace when it comes to gossip? We assume the best about each other and protect each other. It's one of the highest values at my work and in my family. When one of my kids speaks ill of one of my other kids, I shut it down every time because I never want an unsafe culture in our home. **If a culture feels unsafe, then you have no place to thrive, no place to share your issues, your weaknesses, your failures. You have no place to be broken.**

You may be wondering, *How can I possibly shift conversations with my friends to create a safe culture?* I believe you've got to sit down and build ground rules. The healthiest cultures, the healthiest friendships I've been in always have ground rules.

So how do you do this? As you know, I believe in awkward conversations. If you want good friends, you have to have them. So sit your friends down and say, "Hey, guys, we've been gossiping and we've got to stop. I don't feel safe with you. I don't think you all feel safe with me. So here's what we're going to do. We're going to assume the best about each other, and we're never ever, ever going to speak ill of other people or of each other."

It might be awkward for a little while, but it is worth it. You will love feeling safe with your people. Trust me. These are the friendships you want—the encouraging, loyal, safe, got-your-back, too-focused-on-good-to-tear-others-down people you want to do life with.

But start by being that person. Refuse to allow gossip to take place in your presence. Just change the subject, or do what I tell my kids to do: ask, "Why are you being so mean?" Call them out. I know this is basic, but I see it happening from middle school to middle age. Life is so hard. Let's have each other's backs all the time.

The Trap of Comparison

This might be one of the enemy's favorite lies. Instead of your depending on the people God has given you to run with, his insidious whispers of comparison compel you to compete with them, to strive to be better than them—or to feel terribly discouraged if you can't. "Team," by definition, celebrates others' successes because we know we need each other!

If we understand the purpose of our relationships, we can choose celebration over comparison.

My friend Callie taught last night at our church, where I also teach frequently. She was glowing and brought such an incredible word to the women. Not one part of me compared myself to her as a Bible teacher. I took joy in cheering on a teammate who was up at bat.

Because it's brave to lead, to stand up and share your soul, and because I wanted her to not miss how brightly God shone through her. So I live texted her during the whole message, thinking she could read it later as she went to bed. When I hugged her after the event, she said, "Your texts were blowing up my phone during my whole talk." She had her notes on her phone! Oops.

You know what? Let's go down like that, blowing up people's lives to the point of distraction as we tell them all the ways they are killing it.

I know women have a reputation for being petty or competitive. But we don't have to be. In fact, when I look around, I see the exact opposite! From my two sisters, to the huge sisterhood of IF:Gathering, to the women I work with every day, to my incredible friends, to my daughters, **what I see everywhere is women cheering for one another, propelling each other forward, laying down their lives to make their world better.**

My heart swells as I think of all the ways you shape your places through your faith in God, your optimism as you lead, your unselfish dreams, your joy as you create. If you feel competitive with others, ask yourself why. And then choose instead to blow up someone's phone celebrating their efforts. It will start to change your perspective.

The Trap of Laziness

We recognize the isolation of our daily lives, but we don't want to risk rejection or do the work of finding a way to connect. So we don't bother reaching out to anyone—and we wonder why we don't have friends.

It takes more work to have connection than we often are willing to invest. In her book for the Barna Group titled *Wonder Women*, Kate Harris cited a large study of women who are juggling work and family and friendship, noting that "the research consistently shows friendship near the bottom of priorities and time commitments for all women," while at the same time more than one in three women agreed with the statement "I am often lonely."[2]

To have deep, true friendships, we must initiate. We first need to be the friend we want others to be.

Do you want deeper friendships? Do you feel left out?

Quit waiting for people to reach out to you. Start initiating.

And maybe if we are the ones to go first, people around us will feel the freedom to meet us halfway. Assume people want to be your friend. Need things from others and assume they want to help! Ask people the questions you wish they'd ask you.

Pick up pizza and pop by a friend's house tonight. Worst-case scenario, they're busy and you'll have leftovers.

Risk. Need. Bother. It's called community.

The Trap of Fear

One of the fun things about our move to Dallas was that we as a family were all in it together, all nervous, all making new friends, all finding our way around, all trying new places and new things.

It's easy to form snap judgments, self-protect, decide too quickly how you feel about a place or people. But in my experience, you tend to miss the good parts when you operate that way.

It's risky to go through life heart wide open to what God has, to love people without critique or guardedness, to put your whole self out for people to know but also to judge. Yes, it's risky. But in return you get friends, you believe the best, you find an imperfect church community, you get to be imperfect yourself. I'd rather live heart first than guarded, even if that means I bleed more.

Why would we brave this thing that could hurt us so deeply? Because it is obedience. **Commitment and submission to a small local group of people is God's best way.**

When we joined our small group, it wasn't just to have a few friends; it was to submit and commit to a few people. Submission is the only thing that interrupts our egos and tells us the truth. I need someone every once in a while to grab me by the collar and sit me down.

You may hate the church because of leaders there who abuse power or abuse people. I get it! I've been burned more than once in ways that have made me want to run, but likely those leaders were not truly in submission to the structures God laid out.

As a spiritual leader and as a follower of Christ, I am in submission to a board, the elders at our local church where we are members, my husband, and our small group. I realize that, about now, you may be reeling from how that all sounds, but I do this willingly and with joy. Why?

Because, yes, it's hard to trust people—but I don't trust myself! I will start thinking highly of myself, hurt people, and go my own way. I love submission because I know it protects me. We have far more to fear in going it alone than in committing ourselves to go deep with our trusted few.

A Word on Toxic Relationships

That said, what do we do when we find ourselves in a toxic relationship? I interviewed consultant, psychologist, and prolific author Dr. John Townsend during the first season of my podcast, *Made for This*, specifically to ask him if "setting boundaries" was a selfish act or a spiritual one. You'll probably recall that John was half of the writing duo (along with Dr. Henry Cloud) for the groundbreaking book *Boundaries: When to Say Yes, How to Say No to Take Control of Your Life*. The book sparked a cultural phenomenon after its release more than thirty years ago, selling well over five million copies and forever changing our approach to human interactions.

"Jennie," he said in response to my question, "as believers we are quick to focus on all the Bible verses that tell us to love the Lord and surrender our selfish desires and read the Bible and so forth, while at the same time totally neglecting the ones about being careful to guard our hearts, as Proverbs 4:23 says to do. But without guarding our hearts, we will be no use to anyone. Any relationship that drains you faster than it pours into you isn't a friendship; it's a ministry opportunity."

Yep.

Given what I've observed from reading comments on Instagram about relationship and from talking to countless hurting people in real life, my advice for when you find yourself in a truly soul-crushing, toxic relationship is to set clear boundaries, sometimes ones that dictate very little contact with the other person.

Yes, Jesus said to forgive people seventy times seven, which is all but infinite forgiveness. However, we need to be guarded about who we bring into our closest circle. As we've discussed, all of us hurt others at times, but that doesn't mean we have to put our hearts in the path of someone else's ongoing pattern of relational destruction.

Own your part and your mistakes.

Seek reconciliation multiple times.

Don't be afraid to move on if nothing ever changes.

When you know it's time to move on from a friend, I challenge you to be honest and clear, not just ghost them. Sometimes, it's not a close enough friend to warrant that conversation. But if this friend has been a big part of your life, someone that you have trusted and gone deeper with, say the hard thing that needs to be said. An honest conversation about why the friendship needs to end could propel them to recognize where they need to grow and change. It might even repair the friendship.

That said, abandoning relationships every time we run into a problem isn't healthy either. I'm concerned that our impossible standards for who we let in and who we trust stop us from ever letting anyone in.

If we want community, we have to be willing to fight for it.

This Is Going to Take Work

There was a time when what we now call *intimacy* was just called *life*. For centuries, the people you lived near were the people you worked with, the same people you raised your kids with, the same people you worshipped God with, the same people you cooked and ate meals with, and on and on. Daily life meant one continual opportunity to bump up against people, have your sin called out, disappoint a friend, and resolve conflict with a fellow church member.

I look around at our society today and constantly remind myself, "Jennie, you're going to have to *work* for deeper relationship. It isn't going to magically appear."

Becoming and finding life-giving friends is the goal, and the path to reaching that goal is fairly straightforward:

- Ask deep questions.
- Listen.
- Tell people what you are grateful for in them.
- Share the real stuff.
- Talk about Jesus.
- Do fun stuff together.

We all want to become life-giving friends, but in addition to all the traps we've already discussed, we have to accept our own tendency to self-sabotage and drain the life from our friendships. Here are just a few of the self-defeating traps we lay for ourselves:

- Wait for friends to call you.
- Be easily offended by your friends.
- Have lots of opinions about your friends' lives.
- Assume your friends are mad.
- Talk negatively about your friends.

- Don't share your hurts.
- Remember and hold on to friends' mistakes.

If you have been hiding from intimate relationships because you are convinced that nobody wants to be your friend, then might I put on my big-sister hat for just a moment and tell you to go pay someone to be your friend? I mean it. Save up a few dollars and get yourself in front of a counselor worth her degrees. If every single person you have ever been friends with has wronged you somehow, then the common denominator here might just be you.

I know that's hard to read.

Trust me, it's hard to say.

But the truth is always difficult, until it absolutely liberates your life.

Whom do you need to make amends with?

Whom have you given up on too easily or quickly?

Whom have you pushed away?

Whom have you ghosted?

You may have isolated yourself from the very things God wants to use to help you grow. Family, friends, church, small groups—yes, they hurt us, but they are part of the village community we were designed for. I don't want you to miss them because they need some work or maybe they need another chance. We need each other. We need a group of people committed to each other and committed to Jesus to run with and to call us out.

Two weeks ago, I met with a couple of friends to catch up, and partway through our conversation, I risked saying something that was really candid and raw. I told the truth about a situation I was going through, and in response, I didn't feel heard. In fact, one of those friends not only didn't listen well but she one-upped my pain. Have you ever had this happen? You say that something is really hard in your life, and the other person responds by telling you about something she is dealing with that is even harder?

It stung.

Really stung.

And yet by the grace of God, here is what I thought: *She didn't mean to hurt me. And the fact that she was insensitive to my update doesn't mean I should quit telling the truth with her. She is dealing with some super hard things right now—that is factually true. What I can do right now is give her the listening ears I wish I'd had. My turn will come soon enough. I'm going to let this whole thing roll off my back for now and focus on being a friend to her.*

She was probably just having a bad day.

Another friend of mine says that she tries to react to patterns, not one-offs. Everyone messes up every now and then; unless a friend is habitually disregarding or demeaning you, let it go. Choose to move on.

And yet.

If you are noticing that what initially seemed to be a few one-offs has become a pattern of relational misbehavior, might I give you one final word of advice? Before confronting the other person about your perception that things between you are not going well, give yourself twenty-four hours.

Eat something.

Take a walk.

Get a good night's rest.

Pray through how you're feeling.

Then—and only then—invite dialogue with your friend about this downward trend you can't ignore.

I have never once regretted momentarily holding my tongue.

This Is Worth Fighting For

We have to fight to hold on to our people. Let's notice the traps the enemy is using to divide and distract us from healthy relationships. I promise the battle is worth it!

I just returned from a little time with two of my people, Ashley and Lindsey, and I wrote them this text:

> I love us. I love that we get kicked out of restaurants almost every time we go because we stay so late. I love that on one of the hardest days we laughed till 2 a.m. and almost peed ourselves. I love that we talk about everything. We fight for each other to believe truth. We don't hide. We care about paint colors and the state of the world. We move from counseling, to the underground church, to chandeliers with way too much ease. I LOVE US!

Do I say this to brag? Maybe a little. Kidding! Seriously, I say this so you will want this. I say this so you will *fight* for this! I say this so you will read those words and crave your own messy people with your own messy ideas of what it means to be deep, close, connected friends.

Because neither you nor I should be trying to make it on our own through this hard thing called life.

12.

INTIMACY
OF THE FEW

■

*F*OR ZAC AND ME, THE PAST YEAR HAS BEEN EXCEPTIONALLY HARD, not because of anything that has been happening externally but rather because of an ongoing, disheartening inside job.

Specifically, one of our four kids, whose identity shall remain anonymous lest that kid hate me for the rest of his or her days, has been making a string of bad decisions for the better part of four months straight. I should start by saying that our kid has a ton of friends and is intelligent and winsome and can light up a room. This kid is beloved in our family for these and ten thousand other sparks that make their personality distinctive, magnetic, and fun.

All that is true.

What's also true is that kid is making some pretty epic mistakes right now. Mistakes with growing consequences. When anyone you love as much as you love your kids keeps making bad choices, the fear and worry become all-consuming.

I've cried myself to sleep more than once lately, not because of any one incident but because I can't always get my brain to quit whirring over what might happen in coming days if the four-month downward spiral doesn't stop.

That is my hard right now.

If I were sitting across from you at a coffee shop, I would hang on every word you might utter in response to my question: *What is your hard?*

Life is just hard.

People are broken.

Darkness is real.

In fact, I bet if we could find ourselves in an unhurried conversation about things that matter in this life, I would learn of the particular darkness that you and your family have encountered.

You would tell me of the abuse you endured as a child.

Or of the marriage that ended in divorce.

Or about the wayward kid who still hasn't returned home.

You would speak of the addiction.

Or the layoff.

Or the bankruptcy.

Or the diagnosis, the treatments, the pain.

You would tell me about how you thought life would be so different, back when your illusions were still intact.

And in response, I would sit there, legs tucked underneath me, elbows resting on my knees, fingers interlaced, eyes fixed on yours. And I would say, "I know."

Because I get it. Truly. I've been to the dark abyss, too, sinking under the weight of wounds I would never reveal in a book, because the details are not mine to share.

And while maybe I wouldn't be able to *do* anything to help remedy your awful memories or circumstances, **something** about articulating your pain to me, a willing listener, would lighten your load. I would go next, putting words to all my hard. And afterward, the two of us would leave with a bit more energy than when we arrived. Nothing would have changed, you understand. And yet somehow *everything* would be better.

We Need People Who
Are in It with Us

By the time Zac and I arrived at small group after Unnamed Kid's last incident, the other couples in our group already knew. It happens when your small group, your neighbors, and the parents from your kids' schools are the same people. I was tempted to be frustrated by the fact that I couldn't run, couldn't hide from the truth of our situation.

"I've been praying this song for you guys," Elisabeth said calmly. "It says, 'The battle is the Lord's.'" She had her phone in hand, and as she read some of the lyrics, I held back tears.

Then she whispered, "You aren't a bad mom."

My held-back tears turned to weeping. I needed to hear her words. I needed to get my own issues out of the way and do what was best for my kid. I needed my people—people safe enough to face our brokenness head-on, people who are way too deep in all our business, people who know before we even tell them, people bold enough to call out the lies I've been believing, and people committed enough to us and to our kids to help us walk through this for the long haul.

A few weeks later, we woke up to Christmas Day and another difficult situation. My sister-in-law Ashley stopped by, and when she asked about our Christmas morning, rather than pretend we had it all together, I broke down and told her everything. She didn't watch me cry; she cried with me.

As she left that afternoon, I thanked her for being the kind of family and friend I don't have to pretend for. With tears she hugged me tight and long, and she whispered, "We aren't going anywhere. We are in this with you; that kid you love is our kid too. We have this!"

Very few people know the details of our hardest things. I am not exactly an oversharer. But my "few," they know. And they are in it with me.

You and I don't need fifty people to know our hard, but we do need a few who are in it with us.

What I have discovered in finding my people, in building a little village here in Dallas, is that it's not only possible to live this way, it's necessary.

The leader of our way-too-invasive small group is a man in his forties who is married with children. He found Jesus in his twenties and he is a good man. A good dad. A good husband. And a successful business leader.

He *is* all those things.

But you know what else? He's also a sinner redeemed by the blood of Jesus.

I'm not throwing him under the bus here; he would tell you as much himself. And if you were in his small group, as I am, he would tell you much more than that. On a regular basis, the members in our group receive an email from our leader that goes something like this:

Gang, just checking in. Thanks for your continued prayers about [some issue he raised at group last time]. I'm seeing a little victory there, which is encouraging. Still wrestling with materialism. Ugh! It feels like life would be so much better with a little place in the Hamptons. Aren't there better things for me to be thinking about? There are people all around me who don't know Jesus, and I'm obsessing over escaping. Please pray for this beast to loosen its grip.

Also aware that I should dock my phone downstairs at night instead of treating it like another appendage to my body. I've been staring at my phone every night until I fall asleep instead of talking with my family. What am I doing? It's so stupid. I know it's stupid. And yet night after night, I keep making the same dumb choice. Someone hold me accountable, would you? Ready to be not-dumb.

I could keep going, but I think you get the idea. What he models for us is the kind of exchange that you experience only when you are *in it* with someone else. And I've got to tell you, I could not be more grateful that Zac and I are in it with this group.

How Village Life Is Meant to Be

I was thinking recently about how my life would look if I didn't have the net of this group. Candidly, I will admit that from the outside, I would look totally fine. I would seem completely put together, totally self-sufficient, the kind of person who needs nothing from anyone ever. My life would look *good* as independent Jennie, even as inside I would be dying a thousand deaths.

I'd be dying of hard-heartedness.

Guardedness.

Foolishness.

Selfishness.

Despair.

Shame.

As agonizing as it was to walk into group that night and discover that everyone already knew our junk and that there was no getting out of dissecting our junk then and there, I wound up being grateful that I couldn't skate past the fact that I was really and truly suffering. I had no option but to surrender to their love for me, to surrender to my own neediness, and to be the inconvenience I hate being.

What's more, the tenor of that group has taught me how to invite others into my junk. I think of my sister-in-law Ashley, who regularly reminds me that whenever I'm sad, she's sad. Such a simple, straightforward sentiment, isn't it? And yet it levels me every time. Hers isn't a codependent reaction, I should be quick to mention, but rather a perfect embodiment of Paul's word to the wise in Romans 12 about rejoicing with those who rejoice and weeping with those who weep.[1]

I'm convinced that this type of **communal grief and communal joy is what knits hearts together for the long haul.** When you've entered into another person's celebration or another person's pain—I don't mean anecdotally, but rather *truly* entered in—no longer do you bother with boundaries and barriers. They are yours, and you are theirs.

So find your few and let them know they are your few.

One of my favorite things to do is spend time with college girls because college can often be a case study for mile-wide-and-inch-deep friendships. My friend Hannah came home recently after her first semester at college having connected, in typical Hannah fashion, with pretty much everyone on campus. She'd made friends with everyone in her dorm. She'd made friends with everyone in her classes. She'd made friends with everyone in every club she joined. This equated to roughly 53,742 people she now considered her friend.

When she arrived home, she was burned out, exhausted, and sad. "I don't know what I'm doing wrong," she told me one night. "I've been nothing but inclusive with everyone, and yet I feel like I have no close friends."

I looked at my weary friend and said, "Hannah, if you were getting married this year and had to decide today who would stand beside you in your wedding, who would you choose? Who of your closest, best girlfriends could you picture there at your side?"

She wasted no time rattling off five or six names and then looked at me expectantly, not having put things together yet. "Do you think those girls know that they're that special to you?" I asked.

She fell silent for a beat. Then she whispered, "I don't think they do."

I told her that she didn't need to squelch her naturally outgoing personality. "Just be sure you are prioritizing," I said, "the friendships that matter most." I encouraged her to set up some sort of schedule if she had to, to ensure that days, weeks, and certainly months didn't go by without her enjoying meaningful touch points with those wonderful, ride-or-die pals. "Those friends are your anchor, your rootedness," I said to her. "They will give you the fuel—and the accountability—you need to head back out on campus and see who else you can befriend."

After Hannah returned to school, she sat those friends down and said, "I want you to know that you are incredibly special to me. You're my closest friends." Those girls then told the truth to Hannah, explaining how her constant pursuit of more friends made them feel like they weren't a priority to her.

Like many of us, she had unwittingly created not a village but an outright city. She needed to scale things back a bit.

So, that's the first caution: don't go friending the whole freakin' world. Your intimate few are called a *few* for a reason; you need only a handful of them. But the second caution is equally vital: yes, don't befriend a million people, but also, don't hole away.

We aren't meant to carry the problems of the whole world all day every day. But we are the first generation to know them all. Let me be clear: I'm not saying we put our heads in the sand and get a pass to not care about the issues of our day. But in trying to care about everything, we end up helping nothing. It's called compassion fatigue. The people closest to us are falling to the wayside while we bleed out for global crisis. And we end up paralyzed. God set us in villages for most of all time to care for one another—and that capacity rarely exceeded thirty to fifty people in a lifetime. And we've lost that way of life.

For a time, I thought the primary reason for fostering intimacy in at least a few key relationships was so that I would have some people to turn to when the hard times showed up.

But the longer I journey along, the more I realize that the hard times are already here. Every day of every week of every year I live, there is something that feels hard. I'm not trying to be morbid here. Equally true is that on every day of every week of every year I live, there is something beautiful too!

When Zac and I were leaving that small group gathering the night when I had to talk about all the latest troubling goings-on with my kid, one of the other women looked at me and said, "Friend, I know you already know this, but I feel compelled to remind you: when I pray for your family, I pray like I'm praying for mine."

They are ours, and we are theirs. **We belong to each other. This is how it is supposed to be.**

The Very Dearest Friend

Come close and let me tell you something. I realize it's entirely possible you have made it nearly to the end of this book and you still would give your right arm for just one of these types of friends in your life.

I understand. That was me, there on the wood floor of my new house in Dallas. And then Caroline walked through my front door, a college student young enough to be my daughter. I could have seen her only as our babysitter, but I didn't. I saw her as part of our family and eventually part of my circle, my people, my friend. In fact, we were just texting today as I have been writing.

I'll say it yet again: your people might be right in front of you. But even if they aren't today, let me tell you the greatest news:

the one friend I have found to be most consistent, the one who sees me at my worst and still loves me, is Jesus.

And if you know Him, He calls you His friend: "I no longer call you servants, because a servant does not know his master's business. Instead, I have called you friends."[2] That longing we have to be fully known, fully accepted, on mission, seen, loved, not alone—it is wholly answered in Him. Jesus is my best friend.

Maybe you aren't there yet with Him. That's okay. When Kate was five years old, she was telling us about her best friend when her punk older brother shamed her by saying, "Jesus is supposed to be your best friend."

She responded, "Well, I am just getting to know Him."

If that's you, that's okay. But I can tell you this: Jesus makes the *best* best friend. He has never ignored me, cut me out, shamed me, or rolled His eyes at me. Not once. He always listens, always cares, always tells me truth. He is always there. He is safe and encouraging and always challenges me and makes me better too.

You are never alone. You have Jesus. And He has you.

But He wants more for you. More for us. A team of people to run with each day, to love Him together and love each other through the hard. He wants this for you. I want this for you.

It's worth the fight. Run on. Love on. Find your people, and never let them go.

A PRAYER FOR
TRUE COMMUNITY

■

I WANT TO END THIS BOOK WITH A PRAYER. WITHOUT GOD
helping us find our people and keep them, the challenge of
finding and keeping our people feels too daunting.

Please pray with me . . .

God,
We need You. There is no other hope but You. We are
trusting You afresh or maybe for the first time.
Jesus, You were enough for our sins. Thank You that
You made a way for us to first be right with God and
second to be right with each other.
Thank You that You dwell with us.
Thank You for giving us a purpose beyond ourselves.
Thank You that You have not forgotten us.
Thank You that You are preparing a place in heaven
for us to be with You forever.
But in the meantime, we want heaven to come to
earth. We want Your kingdom to come to earth! And,

God, You say that we are the ones to bring it! The
Church carries the hope of Your kingdom to
the world.
So, God, would You heal our broken relationships?
Would You help us to live this?
God, will You help me personally find deep commu-
nity? Help me make friends and keep them as I live
out my commitment to You:
I will build my village and Your Church.
I will play my part.
I will be honest.
I will restore.
I will pull people close.
I will stay.
Your Word promises we can heal, we can forgive, we
can overcome the divisions that threaten to destroy us.
So may we be faithful to believe that and to
fight for it.
God, give us a vision and a hope that is bigger than
our human limitations. May Your kingdom come,
Your will be done on earth as it is in heaven.
Amen.

THE ANSWER FOR
YOUR RESTLESS SOUL

■

*A*s LONG AS WE ARE ON THIS EARTH, WE WILL ACHE FOR SOME-
thing bigger, because we were designed for something
bigger—something better. We are designed for an intimate
relationship with God forever.

Saint Augustine said, "You have made us for yourself, and
our hearts are restless until they find their rest in you."[1]

Humanity had a perfect relationship with God until sin
entered the world through Adam and Eve. With sin came the
certainty of death and eternal separation from God. The pen-
alty had to be paid. But at the same moment that He named
the punishment for the first sin, God issued His promise to
provide a way for us to return to Him.

Our sin was to be placed on the perfect sacrifice. God
would send His own blameless, perfect Son to bear our sin
and suffer our deserved fate—to get us back.

Jesus came, fulfilling thousands of years of prophecy, lived
a perfect life, and died a gruesome death, satisfying the pay-

ment for our sin. Then, after three days, He defeated death, rose from the grave, and is now seated with the Father.

Anyone who accepts the blood of Jesus for the forgiveness of sin can be adopted as a child of God. To each one who believes, God issues His very own Spirit to seal and empower us to live this life for and with Him.

We were made for God, and He gave everything so that our souls could finally and forever find their rest in Him.

If you have never trusted Christ for the forgiveness of your sins, you can do that this moment. Just tell Him you need Him and tell Him you choose to trust Him as your Lord and Savior.

ACKNOWLEDGMENTS

■

*Y*OU CANNOT WRITE A BOOK ABOUT FINDING YOUR PEOPLE without a whole giant slew of them to support you. God keeps teaching it to me, and I'm not too proud to say this book would not exist without a lot of help.

First, to my main person, Zac: I love you and you keep the trains on their tracks. I could never do this work without your constant encouragement and support. You make me better, and you unleash me to do ministry in this way. I know heaven will boast of the unseen ways you serve me and our kids so this can be true. Thank you.

To Conner, Kate, Caroline, and Coop: Somewhere along the way of parenting, you became my people. Today each of you are among our best friends. I love you and I like you. You believe in me and you cheer for me. Thank you for that. As you know, Dad and I are your biggest fans, and watching you become godly men and women remains the greatest joy in our lives.

To my family: Mom and Dad, the older I get, the more I appreciate your marriage and who you are to me. You are faithful and supportive and forever I am grateful! Carolyn and Randy, you both support us in so many ways. I'm grateful to have you as part of our village these days in Dallas. Thank you. Brooke and Katie (my sisters) and Ashley (my bonus sister-in-law), you three are easily called my dearest friends. The bonus is that you are stuck with me forever as family.

To Chloe: I couldn't do this without you, any of it. God knew and He called you in a way I will never get over. You make this ministry work. You make my whole life work. Thank you for caring about this as much as I do—and sometimes, when I get weary, more. James, Gray, Will, and Brooks, thank you for sharing your wife and mother.

To my IF:Gathering family: I never dreamed of the family that IF would bring into my life. From sisters around the world to an office full of people I love working with every day. In every way this is for you and because of you. You have made so many sacrifices to be my people and help this happen! Jordyn, Hannah M., Amy, Danielle, Caroline, Lisa, Meg, Katy, Kayley, Kristen, Kali, Aly, Hannah R., Traci, and to our fearless leader, Brooke Mazzariello, you are gifts beyond measure. I am so blessed to be on such a glorious mission with such a kindred team. Thank you for brainstorming with me and making this better.

To Parker: Thank you for pulling together so many of my words so I didn't start with blank pages! You are my friend, little sister, and teammate. I'm so grateful for your life beside ours these past few years.

To the rest of my village: I couldn't write this without you. Carla, Liz, Michelle, Ellen, Lindsey, Callie, Davy, Jennie E., and so many others. Thank you for becoming my people so quickly and so beautifully! This book is dedicated to you!

To the Yates & Yates team: Here I am again, thanking you. Nothing about you is half-hearted. You are just all in! It is such a picture of the body of Christ. You spent so much time using your individual gifts behind the scenes to be sure that this is the right message and the best way to display God. Curtis and Karen, you are family to us. And I cannot imagine if we hadn't met so many years ago. Our lives would not be the same.

To the Proverbs 31 team: Lysa, Shae, Madi, Meagan, Joel, your creativity and input helped shape this project. I'll never be able to thank you enough!

To the WaterBrook team: Goodness, from our first meeting, I thought you were too good to be true. You all had bigger dreams than I did (and that is saying something), and you so passionately believed in me. You have given me your all, you have shown up, you have thought out of the box about reaching women, you have supported me, even when I get all crazy on you and change the book at the last minute. I honestly could not ask for a better team: Tina, Ginia, Bev, Campbell, Johanna, Chelsea, Lori, Laura W.

And finally to Ashley Wiersma and Laura Barker: This book would not exist or be helpful at all without your love and commitment to it. Ashley, your research, ideas, and creativity made me believe this was a good idea, and you helped it exist!

And, Laura, you and your editing won't let me settle, even when I want to.

Even though this project involved hundreds of hours of me alone writing, I knew I was not alone. Thank you for taking my crazy calls and caring as much as I do that this be all God wants it to be!

NOTES

■

INTRODUCTION: WE AREN'T SUPPOSED TO BE THIS LONELY

1. Tina Payne Bryson, PhD, "When Children Feel Safe, Seen, and Soothed (Most of the Time), They Develop Security," January 9, 2020, www.tinabryson.com/news/when-children-feel-safe-seen-amp-soothed -most-of-the-time-they-develop-security.

CHAPTER 1: THERE IS ANOTHER WAY

1. Elena Renken, "Most Americans Are Lonely, and Our Workplace Culture May Not Be Helping," NPR, January 23, 2020, www.npr.org /sections/health-shots/2020/01/23/798676465/most-americans-are -lonely-and-our-workplace-culture-may-not-be-helping.

2. Brad Porter, "Loneliness Might Be a Bigger Health Risk Than Smoking or Obesity," January 18, 2017, www.forbes.com/sites/quora/2017 /01/18/loneliness-might-be-a-bigger-health-risk-than-smoking-or -obesity/?sh=32b6a0e725d1.

3. Curt Thompson, *The Soul of Shame: Retelling the Stories We Believe About Ourselves* (Downers Grove, IL: InterVarsity, 2015), 52.

CHAPTER 2: THE CONNECTION WE CRAVE

1. For more on this, read Timothy Keller, *The Reason for God: Belief in an Age of Skepticism* (New York: Penguin, 2008), chapter 14.

2. See John 16–17.

3. Keller, *The Reason for God*, 224.

4. Matthew 22:37–39.

5. Matthew 18:20.

6. Proverbs 27:17, NIV.

7. Romans 1:12, NIV.

8. Hebrews 3:13.

9. 1 Corinthians 12:20, NIV.

10. Romans 12:5–6, NIV.

11. Anne Punton, *The World Jesus Knew: Beliefs and Customs from the Time of Jesus* (Grand Rapids, MI: Monarch, 1996), 50.

12. Eric Bond et al., "The Industrial Revolution," https://industrial revolution.sea.ca/impact.html.

13. This insight comes from a conversation with counselor Dr. Mark Mayfield.

14. John J. Pilch, *A Cultural Handbook to the Bible* (Grand Rapids, MI: Eerdmans, 2012), 59. "Western culture is admittedly highly individualistic. What members of this culture neglect to realize is that such personality types represent but 20 percent of the population on the face of the planet. The remaining 80 percent is collectivistic. Members of such cultures feel so strongly embedded in their group that they do not want to stand out as individuals."

15. "Self-Help, Individualism and the Social Brain," *RSA* (blog), January 12, 2009, www.thersa.org/blog/2009/01/self-help-individualism-and -the-social-brain.

CHAPTER 3: A VISION FOR SOMETHING MORE

1. C. S. Lewis, *The Four Loves* (New York: Harcourt, Brace, 1960), 61–62.

2. Brené Brown, "The Power of Vulnerability," TED Talk, filmed June 2010 in Houston, Texas, www.ted.com/talks/brene_brown_the _power_of_vulnerability.

3. See Revelation 21:1–5; 7:9.

4. Elena Renken, "Most Americans Are Lonely, and Our Workplace Culture May Not Be Helping," NPR, January 23, 2020, www.npr.org /sections/health-shots/2020/01/23/798676465/most-americans-are -lonely-and-our-workplace-culture-may-not-be-helping.

5. Romans 3:10–12, NIV.

CHAPTER 4: FINDING YOUR PEOPLE

1. Ephesians 2:4–5.

2. 2 Corinthians 5:18.

3.   See Acts 17:26–27.

4.   Philippians 3:19.

5.   See Proverbs 17:17; Ephesians 4:2; Proverbs 18:24; James 5:16; Hebrews 12:1–2; 3:13.

6.   Judith Graham, "Good Friends Might Be Your Best Brain Booster as You Age," Blue Zones, www.bluezones.com/2019/02/good-friends -might-be-your-best-brain-booster-as-you-age.

7.   Prakhar Verma, "Destroy Negativity from Your Mind with This Simple Exercise," Mission.org, November 27, 2017, https://medium.com /the-mission/a-practical-hack-to-combat-negative-thoughts-in -2-minutes-or-less-cc3d1bddb3af.

8.   1 John 4:7.

CHAPTER 5: CLOSE

1.   Christopher D. Lynn, "Would Our Early Ancestors Have Watched the Super Bowl?" Sapiens, January 31, 2019, www.sapiens.org/archaeology /history-of-fire-super-bowl.

2.   Rachel Nuwer, "How Conversations Around Campfire Might Have Shaped Human Cognition and Culture," *Smithsonian,* September 22, 2014, www.smithsonianmag.com/smart-news/late-night-conversations-around -fire-might-have-shaped-early-human-cognition-and-culture-180952790.

3.   Nuwer, "How Conversations Around Campfire," *Smithsonian.*

4.   Hebrews 10:24–25.

5.   See Acts 2:46.

6.   "How to Make Friends? Study Reveals Time It Takes," KU News Service, March 28, 2018, https://news.ku.edu/2018/03/06/study-reveals -number-hours-it-takes-make-friend.

CHAPTER 6: SAFE

1.   "How Shame Is Secretly Affecting All of Us with Dr. Curt Thompson," *Jennie Allen* (blog), www.jennieallen.com/blog/how-shame -is-secretly-affecting-all-of-us-with-dr-curt-thompson.

2.   Romans 8:1.

3.   See Luke 7:47.

4.   1 John 1:7, NIV.

5.   C. S. Lewis, *The Four Loves* (New York: HarperCollins, 1960), 155.

6.   Philippians 2:14–15.

CHAPTER 7: PROTECTED

1.   Galatians 6:1; Hebrews 13:17; Ephesians 4:25; Matthew 18:15; Proverbs 15:22; Ephesians 5:21.

2. Proverbs 27:17, NIV.
3. 2 Corinthians 5:17.
4. Hebrews 3:13.
5. Proverbs 15:22, NIV.
6. 1 Timothy 5:20; Matthew 7:3.
7. "How to Be a Healthy Person," *Jennie Allen* (blog), www
.jennieallen.com/blog/how-to-be-a-healthy-person-with-jim-cofield?rq
=cofield.

CHAPTER 8: DEEP

1. "Fertile Crescent," National Geographic Resource Library, www
.nationalgeographic.org/encyclopedia/fertile-crescent.
2. Genesis 1:28, NIV.
3. Romans 12:4–5, NIV.
4. C. S. Lewis, *The Four Loves* (San Francisco: HarperOne, 2017), 85.
5. Timothy Keller, *Every Good Endeavor: Connecting Your Work to God's Work* (New York: Penguin Random House, 2012), 47–48.
6. C. S. Lewis, *The Weight of Glory* (New York: HarperOne, 1949), 46.
7. 2 Thessalonians 3:11–12.

CHAPTER 9: COMMITTED

1. 1 Thessalonians 5:11, NIV; Galatians 6:2; 2 Corinthians 13:11; Hebrews 3:13; James 5:16; Colossians 3:13, NIV.
2. Matthew 26:26–28.
3. Ephesians 4:26, NIV.
4. Romans 12:18, NIV.
5. Lydia Denworth, "How Do You Make or Maintain Friends? Put in the Time," *Psychology Today,* March 30, 2018, www.psychologytoday
.com/us/blog/brain-waves/201803/how-do-you-make-or-maintain
-friends-put-in-the-time.

CHAPTER 10: FINDING YOUR FAMILY

1. Psalm 68:6, NLT.
2. 1 Timothy 5:8, NLT.
3. Richard Fry, "The Number of People in the Average U.S. House-hold Is Going Up for the First Time in over 160 Years," Pew Research Center, October 1, 2019, www.pewresearch.org/fact-tank/2019/10/01/the
-number-of-people-in-the-average-u-s-household-is-going-up-for-the
-first-time-in-over-160-years.

4. For more on this, see David Brooks, "The Nuclear Family Was a Mistake," *Atlantic*, March 2020, www.theatlantic.com/magazine/archive/2020/03/the-nuclear-family-was-a-mistake/605536.

5. Aislinn Leonard, "Moai—This Tradition Is Why Okinawan People Live Longer, Better," Blue Zones, www.bluezones.com/2018/08/moai-this-tradition-is-why-okinawan-people-live-longer-better.

6. Erin Jelm, "Fictive Kinship and Acquaintance Networks as Sources of Support and Social Capital for Mexican Transmigrants in South Bend," *University of Notre Dame Institute for Latino Studies*, Spring 2010, https://latinostudies.nd.edu/assets/95249/original/3.7_fictive_kinship_and_acquaintance_networks.pdf.

7. Romans 8:15; 2 Corinthians 6:16, NIV.

8. Dietrich Bonhoeffer, *Life Together*, Dietrich Bonhoeffer Works, vol. 5, ed. Geffrey B. Kelly (Minneapolis: Fortress, 1996), 36.

9. Thomas Merton, *The Sign of Jonas* (Orlando: Harcourt, 1953), 10.

CHAPTER 11: HOLDING ON TO YOUR PEOPLE

1. Ephesians 6:12.

2. Kate Harris, *Wonder Women*, Barna Group Frames (Grand Rapids, MI: Zondervan, 2013), 24.

CHAPTER 12: INTIMACY OF THE FEW

1. See Romans 12:15.

2. John 15:15, NIV.

THE ANSWER FOR YOUR RESTLESS SOUL

1. Saint Augustine, *Confessions*, quoted in John Stott, *Basic Christianity* (Grand Rapids, MI: Eerdmans, 2008), 91.

New Video Study for Your
Church or Small Group

If you've enjoyed this book, now you can go deeper with the companion video Bible study!

In this seven-session study, Jennie Allen helps you apply the principles in *Find Your People* to your life. The study guide includes streaming video access, video teaching notes, group discussion questions, personal reflection questions, and a leader's guide.

Study Guide plus
Streaming Video
9780310134664

DVD also available
9780310134701

Available now at your favorite bookstore,
or streaming video on StudyGateway.com.

Release Your Worries and Fears
and Step into God-Given Freedom

From
JENNIE ALLEN

Available now wherever books are sold.
**Companion Bible studies also available,
sold separately.**

Listen to Jennie's Podcast

made
for this
with jennie allen

iTunes | **Google Play** | **Spotify** | **Stitcher**